Michelle's Dedication

To my Beautiful Granddaughter, Danilla,
who was "Frank's heart."

And … to all of you Beautiful Souls who have been
on this journey of Death and Rebirth before me and
to all who will embark on this journey after me.

I pray that this book will in some way bring you
healing, peace, and comfort. It is those of us
who are left behind that feel the loss.

Our loved ones in Spirit are home in
Love, Peace, and Freedom.

Frank's Dedication
To My Beautiful Daughter Danilla

The day you were born, and your Soul touched mine,
I instantly woke up and knew love. Our hearts became
One heart of love.

Thank you for choosing your mother and I as your parents.
You were the greatest gift I, we, have ever received.
You were born in love. You are love.

Unconsciously, I knew that you and I just had a short
time together on the Earth. Because of this, I taught
you as much as I could so when I left, you would have
a good, solid foundation, which you have.

I know you will always remember how cool it is to be kind.

I will always be with you.
I am one of your Guardian Angels.

I love you forever, Dada

SURFING THROUGH

HEAVEN'S
DOORWAYS

When a spiritual teacher loses her Son,

She ascends into the Heavenly realms
with him and experiences life after death.

Michelle Phillips

Michelle Phillips

Sedona, AZ

(928) 821-2038

www.soulsawakening.com

ISBN: 978-0-578-67529-9

Printed in the United States of America

Editor: Julie Carey

Cover art and chapter design: Mark Gelotte.
www.markgelotte.com

Michelle's Introduction

After arriving in Sweden for my tour in April 2018, I received a phone call that no mother could ever imagine receiving. My son, Frank, had been on dialysis for 8 years, and his heart had stopped while undergoing dialysis. My daughter, Jennifer, was frantic on the other end of the phone telling me Frank was in ICU in a drug induced coma. This is my experience and journey of my son's passing from this earthly dimension into the higher Spiritual realms. Never in my wildest dreams could I have imagined what a Master teacher/healer he is in the other dimensions or the gifts that would come from this horrific lesson, and ... there have been many.

Frank's Introduction

I dedicate this book to all Light Beings / the carriers of the light that have agreed to come to the Earth with amnesia. You agreed to lower your consciousness to match the frequency of the world.

Through your life's journey of karmic completions, the veils lift, and you start remembering who you are. You are magnificent Beings of Light, and as you awaken; you hold the light consciousness for your world to also awaken.

Each one of you are the light of the world.

As your light comes on, you lead the way for all others to come home. You turn the light on for everyone just by being you.

Your world is in a magnificent time of transition. You and your planet are ascending together. You are moving out of third dimensional density and into life after life.

There really is no death. You leave your physical body and move into a higher consciousness of life.

Even though the Earth plane may seem challenging at this moment in the Earth's history, Souls are still lined up to be able to come to the Earth.

The Creator has spoken about the Earth being a hologram where all end times are now playing out at once. You are going through a death of an old consciousness of fear, ego, control and are awakening into the highest consciousness that has ever awakened together multidimensionally.

You are not going to lose your planet as many fear. You are losing the old belief systems of fear.

We are all coming home together, ascending together as One heart of Love. This is happening now on your planet as many of you are awakening and remembering who you are in your physical bodies.

As you know, it was not long ago that I left the Earth, your world, and moved into life after life.

I loved life on the Earth. Earth's life force is pristine and alive.

I suggest you immerse yourself in the life force of your planet. This life force is God, a live consciousness.

As you breathe in this life force, you will be in awe of the magnitude of the Earth's energy.

You are not separate from the planet.

As you breathe in the life force of the Earth's energy, your Soul and Mother Earth's Soul become one energy, one Soul of life force.

You, we, are each other. You are every Soul that walks the Earth, and you are the Soul of Mother Earth.

We are all coming home together beyond any timelines; we are ascending into One Soul, One Consciousness, co-creating Heaven on Earth.

So many of you have completed your karmic lessons, schooling, and are awakening and remembering the higher light of who you are in your physical bodies.

My new work in Heaven's realms is educating and preparing Souls that are getting ready to come down to your planet. There is much excitement in the Spiritual realms as these Souls are now being born on your planet. They are coming down to your world being born fully conscious; there are no veils between Heaven and Earth.

They are the light and future of your world.

Many of you light carriers are the ones who have gone before and opened the light, awareness and higher consciousness for these Souls to be able to incarnate through. You are opening the veils to the Spirit world with the higher agreement, intention, to co-create Heaven on Earth.

I have the gift of being able to educate the incredible Souls that are coming down to your world now. I am also assisting those of you who are already in your world to clear old, karmic emotions, to return to your innocence and self-love.

The intention of this manuscript "Surfing Through Heaven's Doorways" is to lift the veils of illusion so you will remember what is important in life, which is love.

As you journey with my mother, Michelle, into the higher realms, a memory in your DNA will be activated of your higher light and love.

I am honored to serve you and to be of service to you.

Call on me, and I will hold your hand and walk with you on and through your earthly journey, home into the love, light and magnificence of your Being.

I love you. I am you.

In joy, happiness and freedom,
Frank Phillip Peter

Table of Contents

Grief

Grief, I have learned is really just LOVE.

It is all of the LOVE you want to give but cannot.

All of the unspent LOVE flows from your eyes, cracks your heart open, and gathers into the hollow part of your chest.

Grief is just LOVE with no place to go.

CHAPTER ONE

The Day My Life Changed Forever

April 4, 2018

I had been in Sweden for about a week when I got a call from my daughter that no parent can even envision receiving. It was a call that has forever changed my life in ways I am only beginning to understand.

I am a spiritual healer, teacher, author and workshop facilitator. I have spent almost 30 years going back and forth to Sweden.

When I was first invited to Sweden to work, I felt like I had come home. I have many close friends who are my extended family. At one time I was even engaged to a Swedish man.

I was just beginning my Swedish tour and was proud of myself for arriving earlier enough to give myself time to shift through jet lag and to get organized. I was staying in a lovely apartment with a woman who had opened her heart and home to me.

Life felt good, free, and I felt organized and right on track for my tour. All of that changed in an instant when I answered the phone. My younger daughter, Jennifer, was on the other end of the call. She was hysterical, and I could not understand what she was saying.

I said to calm down, take a deep breath, which she did, and then blurted out, "Frank is in intensive care. He was in dialysis and went into cardiac arrest. He is in a drug induced coma to keep his brain cool."

I went into shock and was shaking so much that I could hardly hold the phone.

My son, Frank, lived in Oahu, Hawaii. My daughter, Jennifer, lives on the Big Island of Hawaii. Jennifer was going to catch the first flight to Oahu and said she would call me as soon as she got to the hospital.

When I got off the phone, I could not think as to what I should do. Usually I can spring into action and am pretty good in challenging situations, but now I was frozen in fear.

As I look back, I think of innocent people who are convicted of horrible crimes because of the way they reacted or didn't react after someone's death.

I could not think of what I should do. Jennifer called me when she got to the hospital, and I remember feeling like a lost child asking my daughter what I should do. She kept saying, "You need to get here, mom."

I looked around the room where I had my books, clothes - everything, set up for my tour. I would need to pack everything up in case I wasn't coming back and have my friend come to take everything to her house. I short-circuited. Where do I even begin?

I remember calling my brother, Dan, to speak to my sister-in-law, Debbie. She manages several medical clinics in Santa Cruz, CA. She explained the coma and the procedure that Frank was going through.

I got a ticket for the first flight leaving to Hawaii the next morning and pulled an all-nighter packing everything up in case I didn't return.

While on the flight to Hawaii I remember crying most of the way. I was meditating, and in the meditative state, I saw a Hawaiian service (a paddle out to sea) where we took Frank's ashes for burial. In the meditation, I also saw Frank in the Spirit world in front of the Akashic record board where he was deciding if he would leave our world and go home into the Spiritual realms (what we call dying) or come back to the Earth.

Because I experienced the paddle out burial, I thought Frank was leaving our world. When I got to Hawaii, my sister who lives on Oahu, picked me up from the airport, and we went directly to the hospital where Jennifer was in intensive care with Frank. The doctor explained that the next day they would lower the dose of medication, and hopefully Frank would start waking up out of the coma.

They did not know what kind of shape Frank would be in. They were not certain he would wake up out of the coma or if he had suffered brain damage.

April 7, 2018
Frank Comes Back To Life

Jennifer and I were holding Frank's hands when he came out of the coma. He looked around the room and at us in surprise and confusion. He asked what happened. Jennifer explained and Frank's response was, "Gnarly." We all laughed and again he said, "Gnarly."

As we talked, we were sure that Frank's brain/mind was totally intact. He had not suffered any brain damage. This was not the first miracle of healing for Frank. When he was little, a six-year-old boy, after his third kidney surgery, the doctors told me that they were sure Frank would lose his left kidney. It was small and could not hold its own, but they were going to wait six weeks before they made the decision to remove it or not. At this time, Jesus came to me and together, through intention, we sent healing energy to Frank's kidney.

After six weeks, Frank's doctor took more x-rays and was shocked that his kidney was fine; it had healed itself. His doctor said it was a miracle. He asked the other doctors to look at the x-rays, and they were all very surprised at the miraculous outcome.

This began my own healing journey with Jesus as my spiritual teacher and mentor. I call Jesus my main man and confidante. From my earliest memories, he has always been with me. Because Jesus showed up and healed Frank's kidneys when he was younger, I was not really that surprised now, but I was very, very grateful that his brain was intact.

Jesus has taught me my spiritual work through my own healing processes. We began with him taking me through healing processes to heal my inner child, and from that healing, I learned how to assist others to heal the child within themselves. Throughout the years, Jesus would take me through a healing process, and when I could feel the shift and healing within myself, I would then have another healing process to help others. All of the spiritual, healing work that I do with others comes from my own healing process; I know that it works. Our spiritual work together continues to evolve today.

My spiritual connection to Jesus is not through a church or religion but from the Christ/Love/I AM presence.

Jesus would come to me in the morning and ask me to walk with him, and he would then take me into the Spiritual realms. Because of this, access to the Spirit world with Jesus, my higher spiritual team, and the Creator/God/Source Energy is somewhat easy for me.

As I said, I have experienced a healing miracle from Jesus for Frank before, and I am so very grateful for this one.

Frank's doctor said he has only seen one other person come out of a coma from cardiac arrest with their brain totally intact, with no brain damage. That person was a young man who worked out constantly and was very strong and vital.

When the news had flooded social media of Frank being in a coma, prayers and love were coming in from all over the world.

Frank was a surfer and had surfed and traveled to many places in the world. People loved hm. He was love and always saw the highest in people. He was fun and very easy going. Frank and I had the same spiritual connection ... Jesus was also his man. Frank loved Joel Osteen and his positivity about life and God being a supportive God.

Frank and I separately would watch Joel's Sunday service, and then he would call me and we would share how the message affected us and how it was always what we needed to hear that day.

I don't remember Frank ever saying unkind words about people. If any of us were negative, he would immediately shift the conversation out of the negative and back into the positive, into the higher essence of God/Spirit.

Frank savored life and absolutely loved it. His first love was the ocean and nature. When his daughter, Danilla, was born, his heart opened to a level of love that he could not have imagined to be possible. She was his heart, his love, his life.

In 2010, eight years prior to Frank going into cardiac arrest, he had been out surfing and was having a hard time breathing. When he came in from the water, he went to see a doctor friend of his. The doctor told him that his blood pressure was dangerously high, way off the chart and he needed to go to the hospital and get checked out immediately.

His friend called the hospital so that he would be admitted at once. After doing tests, Frank was told that his kidneys had closed down again and that he needed a kidney transplant and also a heart transplant. But only one transplant would be allowed!

I was with Frank after he was released from the hospital and was assigned a cardiologist. The doctor told him "This is a fight for your life, Frank. You will never be able to surf again, and you will not be able to work as a carpenter." Carpentry had been his trade for many years.

Frank continued to surf, and I remember thinking that if

he goes, he will go doing what he loves most in his life: his connection to the ocean, which is his meditation with God/ Spirit, the Source.

His love for his daughter healed his heart. He told me that he would bring her and his love for her into his heart, and his heart healed.

His kidneys were still suffering, and he had been on dialysis for eight years, which is where he was when he went into cardiac arrest.

Before my Sweden tour, Frank kept telling me that he could feel his kidneys healing and that he was actually peeing more. He believed if he could heal his heart with love, forgiveness, gratitude, and his love for his daughter, Danilla, with Jesus and his spiritual team, he could certainly heal his kidneys.

Jesus had healed him before. He was alive from a miracle. Frank had also shared with me that if he had not gotten sick, he would not have healed spiritually on the level that he had. He was so very conscious about what is important in life.

Here we were experiencing another miracle. He was in intensive care; he wakes up, and we were laughing and celebrating together.

After a few days, he was moved out of intensive care and into the regular hospital. He kept sharing with me how grateful he was to have another chance at life.

He said he was really going to go for it, get healthy again, and have a normal life. I was with him every day, and we were walking up and down the hallways a few times a day so he could build his body and strength up again. I was also massaging his back and ribs. He had broken ribs from the paramedics pushing so hard on him to bring him back to life.

As I look back, I savor those moments of being able to touch him every day.

We shared with Frank how many people had called and all of the love and prayers that were coming in from around the world. Frank was very emotional, overwhelmed and vulnerable from so much love and support coming in for him. He had not known until now how much he was loved, how much people loved and cared for him.

I was in the hospital room when his father called to see how he was doing. Frank was very emotional when he told his father how much he loved him, and his father responded back how much he loved Frank. Those were the last words that they would ever say to each other.

I was very surprised that they had never shared that they loved each other. My side of the family always shared how much we loved each other. We would always say I love you before hanging up the phone or leaving each other in person. After Frank was moved into the regular hospital, his daughter, Danilla, was brought to the hospital to see him.

We had not told her that Frank was in a coma. We were waiting to see what the outcome of the coma would be, and it was very, very positive. After the visit, Frank was so happy to have her and his family with him. Frank said he really did not want her to see him like that in the hospital again and that he would be home in a couple of days. That visit was the last time she would see her daddy alive.

Other than Frank's pain from his broken ribs, he was feeling fabulous and ready to move on with his life.

A couple of mornings after being moved to the main hospital, I was going to see Frank and a nurse stopped me and said Frank had been a rascal that night and was going to sign himself out of the hospital.

I asked if there was a doctor around who could talk to him. It was early morning, and doctors were making their rounds. She said she would find the doctor and see if he would immediately go to Frank's room, which he did.

While talking to Frank before the doctor arrived, he shared that he believed he had been misdiagnosed; he felt great and wanted to go home. Because he didn't remember being in a coma, I think he thought he had just had a nice rest. One of the side effects of dialysis is not being able to sleep, and while Frank was in the coma, he had been asleep for a few days and felt very rested.

When the doctor came in, he explained to Frank that he had gone into cardiac arrest and had passed away. Frank was shocked, emotional, and once again feeling very grateful to have another chance at life.

Because he had been very drugged, he had been confused and because he was feeling so well now, he could not quite understand what he had just gone through.

The doctor was very kind and patient. He strongly suggested that Frank have a pacemaker put alongside his heart so if he went into cardiac arrest again, it would kick his heart back into rhythm.

Frank said he wasn't opposed to having that done, but he wanted to wait a while because he was having a hard time breathing. He had asthma and was just coming out of pneumonia.

The doctor assured him that it would not be a problem, that it was just a simple outpatient procedure. Frank still wanted to wait, but his doctor, sisters, and I talked him into it. He was going to have the procedure the next morning and would be going home the day after that. In two days, he would be home.

CHAPTER TWO

The Day Frank Died / His Second Death

April 13, 2018

The next morning before Frank went in for his simple, outpatient procedure, my sister, Melody, myself, and my daughter, Tricia (who lives in California and had come to Hawaii to help Frank when he got out of the hospital) were all in his hospital room.

The doctor came in the room, and we were all so joyful. I was calling the doctor Our Special Angel.

He was again sharing what a simple outpatient procedure it was. Frank and Tricia were excited that Tricia would be staying for two weeks and they were going to walk every day so Frank could become strong again. They were also happy they got to spend time together, which they had not done in a few years.

I told Frank that I would not be at the hospital when he went in for the surgery, but I would be there when he came out. Tricia and I had been cleaning Frank's apartment so he would come home to a new beginning, a new life.

We had bought him new dishes, new towels, and had thrown all the old out so he would really be coming home to a nice, clean, new beginning.

I wanted to get this all done before the next morning when he would be released. Frank had gone through a few outpatient procedures before with no one at the hospital with him so we all agreed he would be okay to go in by himself, and we would be there when he came out.

Tricia and I were at Frank's apartment when he called before he went in. We were all very happy, laughing, and he was grateful to be coming home to a clean, new beginning. He was calling because he wanted me to bring him a foot-long chicken sandwich. We laughed, and I said, "Are you sure you will be able to eat that after the surgery?" He said, "No problem." He would be starving. We once again shared that we loved each other, and I said, "I will see you in a while. Tricia and I will be at the hospital when you come out." Those were the last words that we spoke to each other.

The next call I got was from Frank's doctor. He asked me if I was at the hospital, and I explained that I was at Frank's apartment. He said, "Would you please sit down." He said, "Frank has passed away." Tricia started screaming.

The doctor then explained that Frank was allergic to the antibiotic they gave him, and he couldn't breathe. I said, "Oh my God. That's what he was afraid of!" and the doctor replied, "Yes, I know, but from a medical standpoint, I would suggest doing the same thing." Frank knew what was best for him, and I listened to the doctor instead of my son. I felt guilty. Why had I not listened to Frank? I asked the doctor to please have his body taken back into his room.

When we got back to the hospital, Frank's body was in the room waiting for us. He looked so peaceful with his hands folded over his body. I held his hands, and his body was still warm. He didn't look like he had died; he just looked like he was asleep or meditating. We were waiting for my daughter, Jennifer, to come back from the Big Island so she could say goodbye to him

My daughter, Tricia, my sister, Melody, Frank's ex-wife, Monica, and myself were all in the room with him. We all felt the same, like he was just asleep and would wake up any minute. His presence was with us, and his body was still warm. We kept expecting him to wake up any minute.

Monica looked at me and said, "Do something, Michelle,"

meaning bring him back. He couldn't be gone. His body is still warm, and we felt him with us. She said when her mother had passed, she could feel that the Soul was gone, but we could feel Frank with us.

One of the nurses came in with tears in her eyes. She said two men had been taken down for surgery that morning, and when they heard the code blue, they were all praying that it wasn't Frank. She said Frank had loved life and was happy, and positive, and he loved his daughter so much. She said Frank was always talking about his daughter, Danilla, and that when a nurse would leave his room, they always felt better, happier in some way.

After four hours of being with Frank's body, a nurse came in and said they had to take his body to the morgue. It was a state law that after four hours, the body had to be removed because of poisons releasing from the body. After four hours, his body was still warm. How could he be gone?

My daughter, Jennifer, didn't make it back, but in hindsight, it was probably the best, to remember him still very much alive.

Jennifer had spent many hours in intensive care and at the main hospital with Frank. One morning, she couldn't sleep and went to see Frank about 1:00 in the morning. They had a very heartfelt conversation. Frank was sharing what an amazing life he had lived. I was a very young mother, and in many ways, we pretty much grew up together. Frank said he always knew how much I loved him, that he always felt loved by me.

He also shared how much he loved my latest book *The Creator, Archangels & Masters Speak on the Cosmic Ascension*, especially the first chapter where the Creator is talking about "Death and Rebirth." Jennifer said that she read the chapter out loud to him and that it was such a heartfelt moment of love between them and God.

In hindsight, I believe this was a message to us from him.

Death & Rebirth

I am the light of your Being. We glow together in the center of all consciousness. We have always been. You have never been separate from Me because you are Me.

You began with Me and will return to Me.

I know this lifetime that you have chosen to inhabit now seems a bit challenging. It is challenging because you have stretched your Soul's consciousness to the beginning of your existence as well as the end of your existence coming back home into the One heart of Love, of our One Creation.

You have seen the world through the eyes of your karmic lessons, and now you are experiencing your world and beyond through your spiritual eye; your third eye. All of your eyes are blending together and shifting you into My eyes and heart and into the larger picture of Our One Creation.

You are now experiencing Me through Our One heart. This is somewhat challenging because Our One heart is constant ebb and flow. In Our heart's eye, there is nothing to hang onto. There is constant shifting; shifting of our belief systems, of patterns, and of your old, karmic foundations.

As you look at the cycles of your world, there is not one sunset or sunrise that is the same. The seasons of your world are constantly shifting. Have you ever seen one summer, winter, spring, or autumn that is the exact duplicate of its last season? It does not exist. Every season is constantly dying and rebirthing itself. Summer, winter, spring and fall do not stop to think about what they are going to do when its season comes around again.

They go with the flow of life: Death & Rebirth. A season does not feel bad, rejected, hurt, abandoned or pass blame that people like it best. It is the season of Creation, just as your Soul has the seasons of Creation within you.

Life cycles will always take you through Death & Rebirth. Your Soul's rebirth now is the birth of your reincarnation into this lifetime. Through your lifetimes, you will experience many of your own cycles of Death & Rebirth: death of belief systems, death of relationships, death of children, death of the way things were or the way you want them to be. Death of your hopes and dreams, death of your ideals, death of beliefs of religions, and always, always, always a rebirth of your Soul's next learning experience.

Your children, loved ones, and relationships that may have left you went into a rebirth of their Soul's next lessons, which catapulted you into the birth of your next lesson.

Your children and loved ones came home into Spirit to be back into the heart of love.

They did not leave you. They will always be part of your heart. Their departure opened a portal of light (It may not seem like light at the time.) for the next step of your Soul's journey. The next step may be to experience grief and loss that you could not imagine to be possible. As you move through the grief, many times you feel anger and injustice, and from this start looking for answers and ways to heal beyond your old belief systems, patterns, or religions.

Many times you took life for granted, and from this unimaginable loss, or grief, you started choosing to live your life — to feel your life — and from this desire, you chose to assist others who have gone through similar situations. Your rebirth led you into your Soul's higher purpose and into the gift of leading many into the light of their Being.

There is no death, just a constant ebb and flow and rebirth of the next cycle of your Soul's journey.

The same experience of Death & Rebirth happens when you or someone you love becomes sick or ill.

You lose your foundation, what you thought was real — another Death & Rebirth of your belief systems, illusions and emotions.

The last death on the Earth is when you physically leave your earthly body and return to Me. Your rebirth will be glorious as the Angels blow their trumpets and assist you home through a doorway of light, of total love, forgiveness, gratitude, compassion and Oneness.

All of your illusional stories dissolve into love. You will experience the joy and happiness of all of your loved ones who have come home into love before you.

You will move into the larger picture of your Soul's earthly journey, and in one instant, you will experience all that you have gone through in its divinity, perfection and love!

The gift of this earthly lifetime is you don't have to wait until you physically die; you can experience the glorious rebirth of infinite love within yourself now.

The veils of illusion are dissolving, and many of you are actually having what you call near death experiences. You are temporarily leaving, and expanding your mental, emotional, cellular and physical body's consciousness into higher dimensions of love. Through this rebirth, you understand that love heals all, and when you move back into Earth's dimensional realities, you are still very open to the miracles of healing — mentally, emotionally, physically — the healing that love expands you into.

Because you are the Cells of each other, you actually open portals of light, of love, for others to expand and awaken into. From this place a rebirth of your dreams and goals shift you into a higher lens of perception and into wanting for your world what you want for yourself. You truly start experiencing yourself as One Cell/Soul of Creation.

Your heart and mind blend into My heart and mind, and together We unfold the collective into higher dimensions of love for all. This love starts shifting your world through the Ascension portals and gives all the opportunity to awaken into love, hope, forgiveness, gratitude, and Oneness. Many of you are having spontaneous awakenings and rememberings of who you are multidimensionally. Every moment, your world's collective DNA systems are breaking down old control systems of greed, fear, and hopelessness.

This is a Death & Rebirth cycle of control. This is creating uncertainty and imbalance. There has always been an imbalance; the veils are just now being lifted. Through intention, as a collective consciousness, you can shift your world into balance.

How do you do this? By staying connected to Sophia, My heart and Me, the Creator. We do not fear; remember, in the higher dimensions, there is only Love. As you and I become One love beyond time, I will guide you back into Heaven on Earth. *

All that you see and experience are old, karmic systems breaking down so that as One consciousness, We can, and will, rebirth your world through the karmic death portal and into a balanced world where the male and female dance together in respect and harmony; where the heart and ego become allies; where love is your foundation and flow; where you allow your and My higher purpose to glide all through the seasons of life's existence and back into harmony and grace; where We sing Mother Earth's song of beauty and resonate with the symphony of colors, sound, and music that Mother Earth so willingly and lovingly shares with us; where We move through all time frequencies and back into the harmony and ebb and flow of Death & Rebirth; where We come home together truly as One Soul of Love.

You are never, ever alone. Call on Me, and you will find a

memory of Our love awaken with you. You have many Masters, Angels, Elders, Wayshowers and Animals that are constantly surrounding your world as We are guiding you and Mother Earth through the Ascension portal back home into Love's Creation.

I love you. I AM you.

Mother/Father Creation

*In my first book *The Creator Speaks*, the Creator explains how his feminine heart opened: "I had discovered My own self-love from the core of My Being. As I continued to surrender in My core, I knew that My heart awakening was My own feminine, My own Beloved, and I called her Sophia. Sophia means My Beloved. The love of my light." (For more information on the Creator's journey of coming into balance with his male and female and all of Creation, refer to *The Creator Speaks* books.)

I think unconsciously Frank knew he was getting ready to leave and wanted to leave us with the Creator's message of Death & Rebirth to help ease our pain, grief and loss.

April 13, 2018
Night of Frank's Passing

The night Frank left this world, I was calling my brother, and my friend Cheryle's voice came on my phone. She had passed away two years before Frank.

I had never deleted Cheryle's voice from my phone's voicemail. She was a big part of our family for many years, and I wanted to be able to hear her voice.

Now, as I am making a call, I hear her voice say, "Hi Michelle. This is Cheryle. I had not clicked on her voice. I knew at that moment, that she was letting me know that she was there to receive Frank on the other side. They had been very close while they were on the Earth together. This was just the beginning of many messages from Frank and the Spirit world.

CHAPTER THREE

The Day the Veils Lifted

April 14, 2018

That night, I was trying to ease the pain of my loss by chanting Ma Ma Ma, a meditation that Mother Mary had given to me a few years prior while visiting the Bosnia Pyramids.

While I was chanting, Mother Mary came to me. She put her arms around me and held me close as I sobbed uncontrollably. I felt so much love and compassion from her.

She said to me, "I know the pain of losing a son. I lost mine while I was on the Earth plane."

Even when we have a deep understanding of our earthly journey, in the Earth's frequency or emotional dimension, this pain feels unbearable. I then felt my whole body fill up with love and peace. I was able to sleep some that night.

The next day, April 14, the veils to the Spirit world opened for me, and I could see Frank with our whole family. There was so much love and joy as they were welcoming him home. Later that day, I saw Jesus with Frank, and Frank was playing his guitar with our relatives gathered around him. I could not hear what he was playing, but loved the fact that Jesus was with him.

Frank loved to play his guitar and write music. While I was in the hospital with him, he was singing a new song that he had written for himself and his daughter, Danilla. Danilla has a beautiful voice and had sung a solo at a play that she was in. There had been about two hundred people in the audience.

I was sharing with Frank about the different father/daughter duos that I had seen singing together on YouTube. He was excited for them to sing together. Unfortunately, I can't remember any of the words.

I was talking to my daughter, Jennifer, about what I was being shown in the spirit world, and she said, "Mom, you and Frank are going to write a book together." At that moment, I received a title: "Surfing through Heaven's Doorways" and was also shown the cover of the book. Frank was surfing through the Spiritual realms.

Before I had left for Sweden on my tour, I remember a conversation with Frank. He was sharing with me what a fabulous life he had lived. He had lived in the most beautiful places in the world. He had traveled a lot and surfed many places in the world. He had lived a great life and had so much love and how having Danilla had opened his heart to love that he couldn't even imagine to be possible.

I remember thinking and kind of chuckling to myself, I hope he is not getting ready to leave, which he was. He was reviewing his life, and I am grateful that he felt it had been a life well-lived.

After his death we were making funeral arrangements, and we found that the coroner would not release the body because the cause of death did not make sense. He needed to find out more of the details of the death.

When the coroner would not sign off on the death certificate, we also decided that we needed to know more about how he died, what the exact cause was. We decided to have an autopsy done to find out the cause of death. It was not offered to us after he died. We reached out to the other hospitals, but no one would do an autopsy. At that point, even the coroner declined to do an autopsy.

A company from the mainland offered to do the autopsy, but we would have to send the body to the mainland, and they would have to embalm the body first. Because of this they were not sure it would be an accurate read.

We then received a call from the hospital where Frank had died and were told that they understood that we were trying to get an autopsy done. They said they would do it, but it would cost us $5000.00. Because this was very much a wrongful death, no other hospital would do an autopsy. We learned how the hospital, morgue, etc. all work together.

Monica decided to do the autopsy because she wanted Danilla to know what caused her daddy's death. It would take about six weeks to get the results of the autopsy.

Monica, my girls, and I then started to plan Frank's celebration of life. We truly wanted it to be a celebration of him, which is what he would have wanted.

We were all in agreement to a paddle out, the vision that I had seen while on the plane from Sweden to Hawaii.

The week of his service was also one of the biggest tourist weeks of the year in Hawaii. It was the Japanese celebration of Golden Week. In Japan, the Golden Week is a series of four national holidays that take place within one week at the end of April to the beginning of May each year. It is considered a time of vacation for the Japanese people. The town was full of tourists and finding someone to cater the event and a place to have the event seemed impossible.

Frank's Celebration of Life

We know Frank then stepped in to assist us. All of a sudden, we had a vision of his service at the ocean. Of course he would want his celebration outside, near the ocean that he loved so much.

We decided to have it at Kaimana Beach where our family had shared so many celebrations through the years. It is also the beach where they celebrated many of Danilla's birthday parties and where Frank had surfed with Danilla.

We also thought that Danilla could go there to talk with and be with her Daddy.

We had his celebration right in front of the ocean. Monica was able to find a company that would deliver a tent, table and chairs, but we could not find a caterer. All seemed to be fully booked. After spending many hours with Monica trying to find a caterer with no success, I was leaving her apartment, and I could hear and feel the words "Da Spot Da Spot" were coming from Frank. Da Spot was a local eatery that Frank loved. I had been there several times with him while visiting Hawaii.

We called Da Spot, and they were available to cater the food; it was Frank's favorite.

We also had the dilemma of finding canoes to take us and his ashes out to sea. All canoes were reserved because of the holiday. Jennifer and I were in Waikiki, and something told her intuitively (Frank) to walk down to the lifeguard station at Kaimana Beach and ask the lifeguards if they knew of anyone from whom we could rent some canoes.

As we were talking to the lifeguards, I really got a sense of Frank's life and the subculture of surfers. They were very helpful and gave us their friend's name who oversees the canoes at the Outrigger Canoe Club. Monica and I had already been to the Outrigger to inquire about their canoes but were told they were booked.

When Jennifer contacted the person whose name was given to us, he said, "Sure. We can help you. Just let us know what time and I will have two canoes waiting for you with two experienced people to take you out."

Frank's guidance was the same way we found a Kahuna — priest/medicine man - to officiate the ceremony, and of course, he was also a surfer, so he understood Frank's love for God and the ocean.

Amy Hanaiali`i Gillioms, one of Monica and Frank's friends, is a very well-known Hawaiian singer, a vocalist, and she was able to sing at his service. Danilla's ballet teacher danced a beautiful hula. She knew Frank because he had spent many hours waiting for Danilla at her ballet classes. She was also a very experienced hula dancer.

With help from above, a very Hawaiian celebration of Frank's send off from this world came together. The celebration of his life was love and joy. So much love, gratitude, and joy were coming from our tent that people walking by the tent would stop and ask if it was a birthday celebration. We replied that it was the birthday celebration of my son moving into the Spirit world.

Frank had sung the Hawaiian song "Kanaka Wai Wai" at my mother's celebration of life two years prior to his leaving. He loved that song and sang it as often as he could. It is a Hawaiian song, and the English words are: Let me walk through paradise with you, Lord. The song expresses how the path to God is found through love and example. We played this at Frank's service, and his daughter, Danilla, and two of her friends danced hula to the song, to her daddy singing his way into Heaven.

My older brother, Mike, did not bring his wife, and I thought it was because she had gone through many losses and funerals and she really didn't know Frank very well. As we sat there in this beautiful Hawaiian celebration of life, Mike said, "I wish Gail were here." As I look back at Frank's send off to his new world, my heart feels full of love and gratitude.

After the beautiful ceremony, we all gathered together to take Frank's ashes out to the sea that he loved so much.

I was in one canoe holding his ashes, and my daughter, Tricia, was in the other canoe. My daughter, Jennifer, who is a paddler of canoes came out in a kayak with one of Frank's friends. Everyone else paddled out on the surf boards. Danilla, Frank's father, and the family were paddling out on Frank's surfboards.

When we got out to sea, the Kahuna blew his conch shell, chanted and said a beautiful sendoff prayer. I then handed Frank's ashes to my daughter, Tricia, and she handed them to Jennifer who was already in the water. Jennifer then took the ashes down to the bottom of the ocean and many who were on their surfboards also went down with the ashes, including Danilla.

As the ashes touched the bottom of the ocean, I was mesmerized as I witnessed Frank rise up, ascend out of the ashes, out of any form, and into his higher self. He was a huge light and was dressed all in white with a lei (flowers) around his neck. He was beautiful and vibrant, the way he looked before he got sick and also the way he was dressed when he and Monica were married.

This is also the way he shows himself to me and others in my workshops. The light, love, and peace that emanated from him was very powerful and healing. This healing higher aspect of Frank was watching over and sending love, healing, and joy to his whole celebration of life. I shared this with others, and it felt like we were in a collective love frequency.

As the surfers were coming back from the paddle out, the ocean became very rough and turbulent. A few of the people on the boards weren't experienced surfers, like my brother, Dan.

Jennifer, who was in the kayak with Frank's surfer friend, Jim, helped my brother back in, and a man on another surfboard was assisting others to get back in safely. I think it was a little scary for my brother who is not an ocean person. He said he would do it again for Frankie.

Once out of the water, Jennifer asked the man on the surfboard who had been helping bring people back in if he knew Frank, and he said he did not. He said he just saw some people were in trouble and wanted to help out. Another man in one of the hotel rooms overlooking the ocean was looking down as we were gathering to go out to sea. He said he could feel the love of the group and took pictures from up above, which he gave to us.

I felt like it was poetic, pictures from up above looking down on this group of love sending a beautiful Soul home, up above and into the arms and heart of a grander love.

It was a beautiful day of love, sharing, and gratitude for a life well-loved and well-lived. A beautiful send off for a beautiful, caring Soul.

One of Frank's friends posted on his Facebook site: Today, one of the sweetest Souls that I have ever met left this world. I thought how interesting that a man would call another man a sweet Soul, but Frank was sweet. He was love.

May 7, 2018

Today has been a very difficult and challenging day for me. I didn't know how I was going to move through my heartbreak of the loss of my beautiful son. I couldn't conceive how I was never going to hear his voice again when he would call me just to say "Hi, Mama. I'm just calling to say I love you."

Even though I have a higher understanding of Spirit, the earthly human aspect of me was in so much pain, and I was so angry with God that I couldn't move into the higher understanding of life, of God, Spirit. I knew it wasn't God's fault, but I needed some place to vent and release my anger and rage.

I kept awakening during the night and was having many dreams of love and acceptance. When I woke up, I surrendered and really asked to be able to move into the higher dimensions of the Spirit world. I was very aware that I could not make it through this loss on my own without God, Jesus or Spirit's assistance. The pain was just too great. I had heard many times people using the expression of being broken. I always felt like people were fragmented but I couldn't conceive broken. Now I felt broken apart and could not understand how I could possibly be put back together.

I have never used the word surrender, but I was actually saying and crying out loud "Lord, God, Jesus, I surrender. Please, please, help me out of this heartache and pain.

This morning Jesus came to me and asked me to walk with Him. As I mentioned, walking with Him to other dimensions has always been our connection, but I was so hurt and angry that I couldn't really surrender until the emotional pain became so unbearable that I had to let go.

I had been waking up shouting, "Show me the way, Lord!" and I knew that was Frank coming through because that was him. He would always tell me that in a difficult situation he would ask "Show me the way, Lord. Show me the way."

As I mentioned surrender is not a word that I have used before. When I talked to my daughter, Jennifer, later that evening, she said she had prayed and used the words: I surrender. Please show me the way. We both laughed through our pain and grief knowing that it was Frank sending us the thoughts of surrendering and letting go.

CHAPTER FOUR

Meeting Frank in the Spiritual Realms

May 8, 2018

This morning Jesus came to me and took me to a place that I was taken to a few days ago: a beautiful garden with a small, white bridge leading to a gazebo in the middle of the bridge. When we arrived, Frank was there, sitting and waiting for us. He was smiling as he was waiting for me. He was laughing and said, "Who would ever have known who the larger aspect of me was while I was on the Earth plane?"

He and I both knew his strong connection to Jesus but did not know how powerful it really was until he got to the other side. Frank and I had the same consciousness on the Earth. We both believed we are of the Christ consciousness, awakening in physical form, and that as an aspect of the Christ's love in our family unit, our purpose was to open the door for our whole family unit to heal.

Frank was laughing so heartily, joyfully, and in great love and gratitude, as he was showing me the great healing, and heart awakening everyone was experiencing since his departure from the Earth's dimension into the higher realms of light. His transition has been a gift to many. He was not laughing at our pain; he was so joyful that his departure had opened the heart of all of us and brought us back together in total love and support of one another.

When Jesus ascended from the Earth, he opened the door to show that life is eternal — that there is no death - that we move into higher aspects of ourselves.

Frank being an aspect of the Christ consciousness, when he left this world, he also opened his family unit's heart to heal, to move through any old hurts, patterns and back into our One heart of love.

The healing that took place from his passing was just that: All relationships that were still carrying hurts or imbalances came back to love. When someone leaves the Earth, a higher doorway of light shines down and gives all of us the opportunity to let go of old, unforgiven hurts, wounds and misconceptions.

Our entire family unit and Frank's friends moved into the higher love. Frank and Jesus were showing me all of this through feeling. Then Mary Magdalene and Mother Mary came to be with us in the gazebo. There was so much love, laughter and joy.

As I looked around, I felt like we were in the true Garden of Eden. Everything was beautiful and alive. The vibrations were very high; everything seemed crystal like. I could actually hear the trees and beautiful gardens humming.

There were so many beautiful gardens of flowers and water fountains. I could actually see the divas in the flower beds. Everything was connected energetically and hummed in a beautiful symphony of love. Birds were also singing, chirping along in harmony.

Then Jesus suggested we all move into the Oneness of Creation, into the One Cell from which we were first created. This is the Oneness that I had been taken into a few days prior when I saw and heard Frank laughing and playing his guitar. I saw all our relatives who were in Spirit gathered around him, while he was singing and playing his guitar for them.

When Jesus suggested we all move into the Oneness, I watched as Frank, Jesus, Magdalene and Mother Mary became child-like and free, light, happy and almost giggly. I experienced myself merge with their energy, and we floated back into the One Cell from which we were first created, into the heart of Mother/ Father/God/Creator.

I felt like a baby of purity and innocence as we all floated multidimensionally throughout Creation in love, bliss, harmony and grace. Such a beautiful love coming together with my son. Everything we had ever gone through on our earthly journey together had dissolved, transmuted, and there was only love and bliss.

We were all light, happy, and free together.

May 9, 2018
Walk in the Golden Field with Mother Mary

I had a hard time going to sleep. The human me was really missing my son, and I cried myself to sleep. I had a fitful night with a lot of nightmares. When I woke up this morning, Mother Mary was once again with me. She asked me to walk into the golden field with Her, the same field that Jesus and Frank had taken me into, the golden field that is my connection to Frank.

When we arrived in the field, Mother Mary started giving me a healing. She started pulling the pain (sorrow, loss, grief) energy out of my etheric body, my energy body. She then sent love, light and healing into my whole body. As she was sending healing into me, she took me back to our experience that I had with her in Bosnia in 2017.

I was at the Bosnia Pyramids sitting in the healing tunnel that led to the pyramids. While I was sitting there meditating in the high pyramidal energy, Jesus asked me to walk with him. He took me through a doorway and on the other side was a large, live picture of Mother Mary. Mother Mary actually stepped out of the picture and started communicating with me.

She was showing me through feeling the crucifixion of her son Jesus and the purpose and impact that the event has had on the Earth. She then showed me through feeling the larger purpose of what Jesus agreed to go through on the Earth.

I could feel her with God-Creator and Jesus and the larger agreement of his death and ascension. She was not telling me in words but downloaded into my etheric body their grander agreement, not the pain of it but the higher purpose of what they had gone through together.

She then asked me to start communicating with Her by chanting softly Ma Ma Ma meaning Mother. After this experience, my whole energy body felt light, clear and crystal like.

Later that day when I shared my experience with my friends and asked them to chant Ma Ma Ma, they all had the same feeling of their whole energy body feeling free, cleared out and crystal like.

In the golden field this morning, as Mother Mary cleared my etheric body's pain energy, she took me into my Soul's higher agreement as Frank's mother on the Earth, just as she had done in the Bosnia Pyramids as Jesus' mother. She then downloaded our larger journey together.

As I lay on my bed after this amazing healing, I was thinking about how every experience in our life is set up for the next step of our Soul's Awakening.

I was once again remembering my conversations with Frank before I left for my Swedish tour. He was sharing with me what a fabulous life he had experienced, how grateful he was, really going into detail.

I think it is really interesting that we have all of these amazing signs along the way. Many times, in hindsight we experience the truth of what they were.

Just like when Frank was in the hospital and was afraid he

wasn't going to make it through the procedure, because he was having a hard time breathing. Subconsciously he knew that he would not be able to breathe through the procedure, and I listened to the doctor instead of Frank ... he knew.

It is really important for us to listen to our own intuitiveness; we have so many insights and feelings along the way ... we know.

CHAPTER FIVE

Frank Reveals Himself as a Master Healer

May 9, 2018

I went to the golden field again with Jesus and Frank. That is our place where we connect while he is writing through me. Today we talked about what happens when we leave this Earth dimension and into the Spirit worlds.

When you leave this world, you will be met by loved ones from your family unit who are already on the other side. They will welcome you so you will have a sense of familiarity and won't feel alone.

Also, the light Beings and Masters who were in your belief systems and religions: God/Spirit/Allah/Christ/Buddha/Yahweh/Krishna, etc. will be the light that opens the dimensional doorways for you to walk or float through.

You get to meet your spiritual team that was assisting you through your earthly journey. Everyone has a spiritual team. Even if it is not your belief system, you will experience that you have not been alone, that you were guided each step of the way. When you move into the Spiritual realms, you awaken into your higher spiritual knowing … understanding.

Since you don't have a physical body, you will experience yourself floating through what feels like timelines. You are actually crashing and expanding through old, karmic timelines and home into the center of your earthly belief systems, religions, etc.

After a time of transition, after you reconnect with loved ones and come back together in love and forgiveness with them, you will find yourself in a dimension of like consciousness. If you were Christian, you will find yourself in the heart of the Christ Consciousness. If you were Muslim, you will find yourself in the heart of that belief or religion. The same is true for all religions and beliefs. If you are Jewish, Buddhist, atheist, etc., you will feel and experience yourself in the center of your chosen earthly agreement. You will shift beyond your earthly agreements and belief systems. You will then be taken through a doorway of light and into a crystal room, the Akashic record room, with Beings of light that will assist you to review your whole lifetimes' agreements.

You get to experience all of what you went through with others through the highest lens of perception. If you are carrying pain, regrets, sorrows, the higher vibrations of love will transmute these unresolved, painful emotions into love and acceptance.

Because there is no past, present or future, during this review you will experience everything at once. You will also experience the feelings from other lifetimes and journeys that you have gone through with others. Through this review, you will know if you completed everything that you agreed to go through with each other in the lifetime that you just moved out of.

In Spirit, there is no judgement of you, only love, compassion, forgiveness and acceptance. After you go through the karmic review board, you will go into a place of healing and rejuvenation of your Soul's spirit.

You actually get to hang out with your loved ones who have gone before. The difference is that you only experience love, joy and happiness with one another. As you shift higher dimensionally, there is nothing to heal or forgive; only love exists.

In the higher Spiritual dimensions, you may see some of the

patterns and obstacles that you went through with others, but there will be no negative, emotional attachments, only love. A great healing and understanding will take place between you and those who went home before you. You will forgive and come back to love with each other.

All of the illusional veils are lifted as you remember who you are. Your higher spiritual team will also be very much with you. Many of you are great light Beings — Masters - who have lowered your vibration to assist many others on the Earth through old, karmic, emotional stories. As you leave the Earth's dimensions and heal painful emotions, you also transmute them for your loved ones who are left behind on the Earth.

May 2018
My Return to Sweden

After Frank's celebration of life, everyone was returning to their somewhat normal lives. I decided to return to Sweden and if possible, finish my tour. I really had no idea what kind of emotional shape I was in or how I would be able to function.

Because I have worked and lived in Sweden for so many years, I felt like I needed to return there. I knew I had a tremendous support system that would love and support me through this "Dark Night of the Soul," which they did. I just felt like I couldn't go back to Sedona, AZ because Frank called me all the time when I was home.

When I went back to Sweden, I wasn't sure if I was going to be able to finish my tour.

I was speaking to a group this evening, and after the earlier events of today with Jesus, Frank and my team, I thought I would go and share my story. My intention for sharing was to help people to open their hearts to the importance of love, of totally being present with others, of living in the moment because you don't know when you won't have that moment again.

I could feel Frank with me. He had said to me earlier in the day, "I have got your back, Mom." I didn't know that he meant literally. I could feel his light energy in my sacrum, up my spine, and expanding across my back and way out above my head, like huge angel wings.

As I was speaking, I could feel his beautiful light energy holding me up. On the break people were telling me that they could see this huge light behind me. Later I shared that it was Frank.

After the break I took people into a meditation and healing process. It always starts with Jesus, Archangel Michael, Mother Mary, Magdalene, Melchizedek and my whole healing team clearing people's bodies. They start by pulling old energies out of their etheric DNA systems, body systems, chakra systems, and brain compartments. After the clearing/healing, your higher self's light and love fills up all of the spaces that have been cleared.

This time I was shocked as I witnessed Frank right there with Jesus and the team working on healing people's body systems.

Frank was pulling old pain and hurt out of people's heart and thymus and then filling them back up with light and love.

I was amazed to witness what was happening. I knew that Jesus had been Frank's main man as he was mine but really didn't have an idea of how connected they were.

After the healing session, people were saying that it was the most powerful experience that they had ever gone through. They said they could feel Frank pulling the cords and pain out of their hearts and his love filling them back up.

After Frank's departure from this world, he had communicated with my daughter that he was going to be working with me and through me. Such a powerful, profound and truly unexpected experience.

And ... we have only just begun!

The whole day and evening was certainly lifting me into the higher dimensions of God, Spirit and healing with Frank.

I felt overwhelmed with love, gratitude, loss and confusion. I absolutely knew and believed this is who I was, who Frank was, and yet, there was still a human part of me that kept going over his last days in the hospital and how his earthly life had ended. He had died two times.

Frank was telling me from the other side to not go into his last earthly days, to stay connected to the truth of who he really is. His life had been about love and wanting to live the Christ consciousness, to truly be it, to make a difference in the world by example. His intention was to assist the world to heal by one person healing themselves and then whole family units would heal.

He loved and practiced Ho'oponopono, an ancient Hawaiian healing practice.

Now he was on the other side and could reach many through his love and healing. He certainly is with the best healing team that I could imagine being on: The Christ — I AM — healing team.

May 10, 2018
Loss and Grief

It is now 3:30 am. I have been awake since 2:30. I have things to help me sleep, but I am afraid that if I take something, I will miss a communication from Frank. I want to be clear enough for him to contact me through a dream or in the golden field.

Last night was a tough one. I have so many emotions: hurt,

guilt, fear, separation, loss and grief coming up. I turned the TV on looking for a diversion. There was a great documentary on about Janis Joplin's life. Being a 60s child, many memories surfaced for me. I kept having flashes of Frank's young ages, what he was like, what he was doing and what I wasn't doing, meaning how unpresent I was in his life.

I flipped channels and there was another documentary about the 80s television. Frank's life went before me again. What was he doing then? How old was he? What was I doing? Way too much pain. I just turned the TV off and decided to will myself to sleep, to see if I could make contact with Frank again.

CHAPTER SIX

Frank Explains His Earthly Journey and His Expansion into His Higher Spiritual World

May 11, 2018

It is 10:30 at night. I should be tired, but I had taken a nap and now I could not sleep. I went to bed sobbing and asked for Mother Mary to be with me, to take me to the golden field to be with Frank again.

She immediately came to me and together we went to our meeting place to meet Frank. He was waiting for me. His energy felt different, more distant, not distant in not being available but more distant because he was so expanded, much larger than the role he had played as my son on the Earth.

He was explaining to me that he was expanding into himself, his light multidimensionally, so he could move into his higher spiritual work. His voice even sounded more expanded. I wasn't ready to lose him as my son.

He explained that he would always be my earthly son and yet his spiritual mission was so much beyond the Earth. I knew he was a very high light while on the Earth. He was love. He left a legacy of love. He had such a zest for life, savoring every moment. He loved the outdoors and surfing. He said surfing was his meditation. When he was in the ocean waiting to catch the biggest wave, he was with God.

As I am in the golden field with him, I am experiencing his energy expanding through the higher realms or dimensions of Spirit.

He explained that his Soul had needed a refresher course on the Earth and that he had chosen me to be his mother because we had been through other very high, conscious lifetimes together. He could also see through the Akashic records that this lifetime for me would absolutely be one of service to God. He could see that I would awaken spiritually as much as I could and that Jesus and the Creator would always be with me, that they would be my guiding lights. Which they have been.

Since my earliest memories as a child, Jesus has always been with me, not necessarily through a church or religion but from the essence of His Christ Being. He actually talked to me, had me walk with Him as He guided me step by step in my Soul's Awakening.

Frank said he knew with me as his mother that he would be able to have a strong connection to Jesus and God, a foundation with Spirit that would guide him through his life and through his departure (full circle) back into the Spirit world. He was very grateful for our journey together.

He said I would still feel the human Frank's energy with me but not on the level that I had for the last few weeks. He was basically shifting gears into higher dimensions of himself, of God, Spirit, to be able to do his spiritual work.

He had gone through an earthly refresher course. Our earthly journey is actually just a blink of the eye in our Soul's larger journey.

I fell asleep feeling love, peace and harmony, yet when I woke up at 2:30am, I felt empty again. I can feel his earthly connection to me, my lessons, and I feel somewhat lost. I asked to go into the golden field, but he is not there.

I am going to facilitate a two-day workshop starting tomorrow and was expecting Frank to come through as he had the other evening.

Again, I think to myself that I don't know how parents get through this loss without a spiritual connection.

I find it interesting that Frank loved my latest book and the first chapter. The Creator talks about returning home, coming full circle. As I said before, I believe that a higher aspect of him knew that he was leaving the Earth and the chapter explains it all, for him and for us who are left behind.

I am finding that writing helps, and I know it is what Frank wants me to do – to tell the story.

Earlier yesterday he had asked me to contact his daughter and tell her to lie on the bed with her hand over her heart and say, "I AM. I AM. I AM with my Daddy." Then take a few breaths and eventually she will feel him with her. The I AM will start dissolving her hurtful, frozen emotions and she will feel him, his love, with her.

Frank loved the I AM. While in the hospital before his passing, he said the clock was ticking and he would chant I AM with the ticking sound, and he would expand into the I AM multidimensionally, then the ticking sound would not bother him.

I know that time is an illusion, but when you go through a loss like this, time seems to stand still and everything is absolutely in the now, the present; every experience, every emotion, every memory is lived all at once. It feels like timelines collapse and all emotion erupts like a volcano spilling over and out paralyzing my ability to function.

I look at my body and see what stress and grief have done to it. At first, I could not eat, and I lost so much weight and most of my muscle tone.

Yesterday, I had the opposite experience. Because I had so much grief and loss surfacing, I kept eating everything in sight trying to numb myself. I have also noticed that food doesn't really have much taste. Everything seems to taste the same.

It's hard to believe it has been almost a month since Frank left. The first two weeks were such a blur, preparing for his celebration of life.

As I was setting up for my two-day workshop. All I could think about was Frank. I was wondering if the pain, the loss, ever goes away. Will my mind ever be able to think of anything else but him?

After my two friends helped me set up for the workshop tomorrow, we sat down to have tea. We could all feel Frank's higher self's presence with us. I witnessed myself laughing as I talked about him and our higher journey together. I actually felt joyful and light and was then able to sleep some throughout the night.

Workshop Day 1: I slept off and on but was able to get some sleep. I feel pretty good, even feel like doing some stretching before I leave. I think I am starting to come back some. Yesterday, I told myself that I would allow myself to grieve a certain amount of time throughout the day. I never know when the emotions will come up so decided to give myself little time slots throughout the day, not long ones but enough to let the emotion come up and out. I also experienced how crazy, how stupid, that intention was. Grief has a mind of its own and surfaces when we least expect it, especially in the beginning of the loss.

Perhaps later on a person can give themselves a timeline daily to experience the painful loss, but in the beginning one must go with the flow.

The first day of my workshop was the toughest. I was processing the group, taking them through meditations, assisting them to let go of past hurts and patterns from parents and ancestors, to be able to move into a new lifetime on the Earth, living from their highest intention for life. This process is about clearing out the past to make room for the new.

All I could feel or think of was that I wanted to die. I am teaching them to live and I literally was thinking and feeling like

I wanted to die. I had overwhelming feelings and thoughts of suicide, and no one or thing could matter enough to make me want to stay. I just wanted the pain to go away.

At the same time, I was thinking so this is what it is like when one takes his own life. The pain is so overwhelming that they just want to disappear. It's not that the person necessarily wants to die; they just want the pain to go away. When you are in this much pain, it is hard to think about those who you are leaving behind.

I wanted to die, to move through the pain, make it go away. I was feeling like I did not want to exist in any dimension. I felt like I wanted to die, be cremated and my ashes taken out to sea with Frank's. I did not want a celebration of my life; what was there to celebrate?

I know my life has certainly been one of service to assist others to heal, which has always been so fulfilling. Many times, after a workshop, I cry from love, to be able to experience another person letting go of their old, painful emotions, to witness them move into a place of forgiveness and self-love is the ultimate high.

I am always very grateful and thankful for my agreement to serve God, to love on the level that comes through me. I am so blessed to have the connection to the love of God, Christ and the Spirit world.

I was always so busy, traveling, doing workshops, but never really took the time afterwards to enjoy wherever I was. I would facilitate great workshops, people's lives would shift, heal and then I would usually go back to wherever I was staying by myself.

I had dedicated my life to God, to be of service but forgot to serve myself what I was offering to others. In my own personal life, I had not taken the time to enjoy the experience of my surroundings. I certainly have had moments of joy, love and laughter, especially with my kids and family. We have a very close family, but I don't live around any of them anymore.

My mind was so split. I was feeling the depth of my suicidal emotions and analyzing what I was feeling, my experience of what it is like to commit suicide.

Driving back to my apartment from the workshop, I could even see and experience the beautiful landscape around me. Sweden is so incredibly beautiful in the springtime, everything coming alive.

When I got back to my room, I was sobbing. God take me. Take me, not him. Take me. I can't stand the pain. It was too much. Let me disappear. I laid down on the bed and did disappear for about four hours.

I went into the pain and was surprised when I woke up four hours later. I still felt the loss but not on the level that I had earlier. I was surprised that I was able to go back to sleep because I had not been able to sleep much. The pain was like a volcano bursting and once the built-up emotions burst, I was able to get some rest.

While in the workshop, all I could feel or think of was that I wanted to die. Like I said, I was teaching the participants to live their lives to their fullest and I literally was thinking and feeling like I wanted to die. I had overwhelming feelings and thoughts of suicide, and no one or thing could matter enough to make me want to stay. I just wanted the pain to go away.

May 13, 2018

It has been one month since Frank left this world. Friday, April 13th. Friday the 13th. The pain of his leaving is just as strong now as it was when he left. The first two and a half weeks were trying to get an autopsy done and then the arrangements for his celebration of life. I didn't really have time to grieve or mourn on the level that I am now because I was so busy, and I also had my two daughters, sister, and Frank's family with me. I am now in

Sweden without family, and the raw emotions of the loss of him are sometimes unbearable.

Workshop Day 2: While facilitating my five-day workshops, I always have people tell their life story. I believe we stay as sick as our secrets, and when we share our secrets in a safe space with others, we start healing. When someone is heard, they can start shifting through the frozen, emotional pain. I didn't know how I could get through another day hiding the way I was feeling, hiding my pain.

I felt very loved and supported by everyone in this workshop. Most of the participants had taken part in many of my other workshops, and we were definitely a Soul family. Because of this love and support, I decided to share the way I was feeling, to tell my story. Through tears, I talked about my emotions, loss, grief, loneliness and hopelessness.

As I was sharing my feelings, I felt myself moving out of the unbearable, emotional pain and into a higher vibration. I was moving out of my collective pain body and into the heart of love. I actually shared love, joy and laughter with the group. I was being reminded again how important it is for us to have a tribe, a safety net, when we are falling. Our tribe will help us back on our feet. I could feel the painful emotions start to drain out of me, out of my root down my hips and out the bottom of my feet.

I knew I had been in the morphogenetic field and quantum field of all who had experienced unimaginable loss but was not able to shift out of the fields until I told my story of how I was feeling. I was then able to move into a higher field of love.

I feel Frank with me, and everything I do, watch, or listen to reminds me of parts of his life.

I feel like I am moving through life with veils surrounding me. I can see but not truly feel the essence of life. I am in a fog looking out. I am trying to eat to put weight back on but don't have much of an appetite. I feel nauseated much of the time and I can't really taste the food.

As I said I had made up my mind that I would give myself time slots to grieve. At this point in his departure that is the most stupid decision I have made. It is still too soon. I cannot predict when the emotions will come up.

While in the workshop yesterday, I was split between my mental mind, emotional pain and feeling suicidal. I was asking Spirit about taking my own life. Their answer was that it was not my time to go - my earthly contract was not up – and if I chose to leave this way I would have to come back to Earth again and complete the lesson.

I was not feeling like a victim; I was just grieving and suffering loss. Again, I was thinking about people that have experienced horrendous loss and don't have a spiritual foundation. I don't know how they get through it. I also realized I was in the quantum field of that loss.

I feel like I am on an emotional seesaw. I also feel that as I am taking people into the higher light aspects of themselves, their light, my light is activating my pain and loss.

The second day of the workshop ended up being very powerful. People said it was the highest workshop that they had ever experienced, that they really felt complete karmically with their parents and ancestors and all they could feel was love, forgiveness, gratitude, and Oneness.

I could also feel Frank working with us, with my spiritual team and everyone in the group's team.

One of the women that I have known for many years said she was having the feeling that she should go to Hawaii. She was being shown a vision of someone dancing hula. She then asked if Frank had kind of a flirting energy. I had to laugh. Yes. That was Frank; he loved life, had a zest for life, flirted with life.

Frank was also very handsome and exuded love, light, and humor. Women loved him and he loved women. He was raised in a female household. He also had a very masculine energy and had great male friends but was very compatible with feminine energy.

I am finding writing is very therapeutic for me. I learned this many years ago but haven't written down my own feelings and emotions much over the last years.

May 15, 2018

Yesterday, May 14, Wednesday, was a really hard day. Thursday, May 15 was a very powerful, euphoric day.

Frank was with me all day and wanted to channel a letter through me to his daughter, Danilla and another one to Monica (his ex-wife). The information was incredible, explaining his whole earthly journey. He was also taking me through our journey together and explained so many circumstances and the emotions of the circumstances that we had gone through together. He explained his feelings at the time.

I didn't have time to write the letters because I am back in Sweden finishing my tour. Because I had canceled much of my tour, I needed to send some mailings out to people to update them.

When I woke up yesterday, I still felt light and euphoric. Frank asked me to please write a letter to Monica. She was having such a difficult time for herself and the pain she was feeling for Danilla. The emotions were affecting her health.

For two days Frank had been explaining to me how sick his body was. He wanted Monica to understand this. None of us really knew his condition because he never talked about it; he didn't want to send negative energy to his condition. He just wanted to focus on the positive. I also think his condition had become his reality and he learned how to live with it.

Now he was sharing with me and really wanted me to understand that his body had quit functioning and that there was nothing any of us could have done. His kidneys quit functioning. He had been on dialysis for eight years. He went into cardiac arrest and his heart quit. He was having a hard time breathing; he had asthma and was using an inhaler. He had pneumonia. His lungs were closing down. He was also having symptoms of pins and needles in his feet and calves.

Although his Spirit was very high, his body was worn out. There was nothing any of us could have done. It was his time to go.

I have worked with, assisted others, as they were getting ready to go home, leave this world back into Spirit and had experienced the same thing with them. I think they are already merging with the higher aspect of themselves, higher self, and they are feeling light, unburdened and freer.

I experienced that with my father before he left this world. I was with him two weeks before he died, and he was like a young man again. He was happy, joyful and his great sense of humor was back. He was talking about us going to Yellowstone Park next year. Two weeks later he was gone.

Yesterday after writing Monica for Frank, I met my friend for dinner. I started feeling very down and depressed, stuck emotionally. All of my thoughts were negative. I was numb, looking at the world, people around me but not feeling it, like from the inside looking out but not connecting.

It was a beautiful summer day in Sweden, so green and alive — everything in bloom and people were very happy to be outside in sidewalk cafes. I was numb, like watching a movie. I was doing my best to be kind, nice, but I felt agitated and frustrated.

I was also realizing that because I had been vibrating in such a high light frequency in communication with Frank that the light had activated another level of my hurt, grief, and painful emotions. And that it did.

CHAPTER SEVEN

Blocked from Death's Doorway

May 17, 2018

I woke up this morning and felt like a dam of loss and grief had burst open. All I could do was cry. Everything and everyone reminded me of Frank. I was leaving today to go to Darlana in Sweden, to speak and work.

I had a four-hour train ride to Darlana, Sweden and cried most of the way. I was frozen in pain, loss and grief. I called in Spirit, meditated, chanted, gave myself a healing and felt a little relief but not much.

When I arrived in Darlana, I experienced it being very beautiful, green and alive. I could see it through my layers of pain but couldn't totally feel it. I wanted to close my eyes and disappear into its beauty — just dissolve, go away.

I was scheduled to do a mini workshop that evening. When I started speaking to the group, I was witnessing myself speak but could not feel any of my energy connected to my words. My mind was saying something, but my emotions were still in grief of the loss of Frank. I was watching as people were taking in my mental gibberish and could feel that they were not really relating to what I was saying. They could not feel it.

I was talking about my last book and the first chapter from *The Creator, Archangels & Masters Speak on the Cosmic Ascension & the Light at the End of the Tunnel* where the Creator is talking about everything being Death & Rebirth.

I then went on to say I had experienced this firsthand as my son had just left the Earth. As I started talking about Frank, I couldn't breathe, literally could not breathe. I could not catch my breath. My lungs were frozen, and my throat closed down. I was choking in front of my audience. I knew I was choking to death. I couldn't shift the frozen energy. I watched the audience watch me as I was choking to death. I knew in an instant that this was the way Frank died. He was allergic to the antibiotics that were given to him. His throat closed down. He couldn't breathe, and he just popped out of his body.

Somewhere inside of me, my breath, the air still left in my abdomen, started moving up through me and into my lungs, and I started to sob, cry. As I turned around and looked at the audience, I saw many people with tears in their eyes. I always want to be authentic when I am speaking with a group, and I certainly could not be more authentic than this.

After that amount of frozen emotion released, I could feel myself lighter. I could breathe much easier. I then made a joke about it; humor really heals and sometimes it shifts us back into balance, which it did for me.

After that authentic show, I took a break, and people were coming up to me thanking me. Then I took people into a meditation that was fabulous Afterwards, people were sharing incredible experiences. People in Sweden don't show or share their feelings and emotions much, so it is really a breakthrough for everyone when they do. I realized that the energy from Frank and the Spirit world with us was very high, and people were vibrating in this awakened frequency. We were very much in the Spiritual realms.

I have had a hard time sleeping, very sporadic, and haven't wanted to take anything to help because I don't want to miss Frank coming through me in a dream.

Before I went to bed tonight, I shared a meal and bottle of red wine with the woman who has invited me to Darlana. She lives in a rustic, wood-built home. It is such a beautiful lakefront home.

Her brother built it back in the 30s and didn't want to live in it, so she bought it from him and has lived in it for thirty years.

It is a beautiful, private space with trees and water all around. We sat in a glass room watching the sunset. Swedish summers are light way into the morning. The sun goes down for a short time around 2 or 3am, but it never really gets dark. Then the sun comes back up again. Unfortunately for the Swedes, the same is true about darkness in the wintertime. It is pretty dark most of the day.

When the light comes, Swedish people don't want to miss a second of it, so they are up celebrating life way into the morning.

As I sat with her in this incredible setting, all I could feel was loneliness, the loneliness that I have felt so much of my life.

I was telling myself, "You aren't alone. You are sharing this evening and great conversation with this beautiful, conscious woman with whom you have so much in common." All I could think was make this pain, heartbreak, go away. I am very conscious of energy and thoughts and didn't want to put energy into the word heartbreak, but the song kept coming into my mind: "How do you mend a broken heart?"

May 18, 2018

As I lay in bed the next morning, my whole life was going before me as it had since Frank left but this was on another level. As I mentioned before, Frank had been talking about what a great life he had experienced. For a couple of years, he had been reviewing his life and kept expressing to me how magical his life had been. As I was continuing to review my life, I didn't feel like my life had been fabulous and fun; I felt like I had grown a lot spiritually. My life had certainly been one of service, but I can't say that it has been fabulous and fun. Since Frank's departure,

I am constantly reviewing my life.

That day I facilitated a one-day workshop. As I look back, I absolutely knew that spirit was facilitating. I was just the spokesperson for Spirit to work through. Once again, it was an amazing healing for those who participated. I just got out of the way and let Spirit come through.

That night, I sat by myself outside of the cottage where I was staying, and I felt depression and loneliness. I was so alone and had no life force. I felt like I did not have the energy to get up and go to bed. As I was sitting there, I witnessed myself get up and start walking down the dirt road in front of the cottage. I was amazed. How could I be walking? I didn't have the energy to even get up to go to bed. Who was walking me?

I continued to walk and came into a clearing in a beautiful forest. I realized Frank and Spirit were walking with me, actually through me. Frank wanted me to experience this majestic beauty through his eyes, through his feelings.

As I stood there, I started to sob and scream uncontrollably. I could not stop the pain and sobbing. It was voluntarily releasing from me. When I was finally able to stop, I could see the beauty in a much clearer way. Some of the veils of pain were gone.

I still stood there numb, but I could breathe a little easier. I then witnessed myself walk back to my cabin. It didn't feel like me walking. Who was walking me? When I got back, I was even more exhausted. I am staying in an old cabin in the middle of nature and across the street from a lake. This was Frank - mentally, emotionally, and physically - he would love it here. He would be hiking, exploring the nature that he loved so much and would definitely be swimming in the lake, even if it was cold. He had such a zest for life and an appreciation for nature. Please Lord, God, let me experience life through Frank's heart and life's energy and vision. It was so much greater than mine.

That night before I went to bed, I had a very surreal experience. All of a sudden, I knew that I was absolutely leaving the Earth, dying. It was interesting because I didn't feel any emotions connected to it. Not love, gratitude, fear, confusion – absolutely no emotions. I was numb.

I wrote a note because I knew my friend would find my body. I gave her my brother's United States number and asked that she call him. I also left a message that I did not want a service. Please take my ashes out to sea with Frank's.

That was it!! My life ... over!

I have heard, read, that many times when a husband or wife dies, a loved one, the other person, leaves shortly afterwards. And I was going home to be with my son.

The wine relaxed me enough that I was able to go to sleep easily and the dream came.

My Dream

In the dream I was going somewhere, and I took the wrong turn. I saw someone selling clothes; I don't care anything about looking at them so I turned the car around and saw a sign that read San Jose, CA. I thought I have no desire to go to San Jose but then think, well I can drive through San Jose and get to where I am going. In the dream I was remembering that in the first part of the dream I saw a woman who was sick, and her son was in the hospital. I was wondering if she was going to go see him. (Frank was born in San Jose, CA.) When I turned to drive to San Jose, I woke up out of the dream.

As I woke up, my mother who is in Spirit was very much in the room with me. The room was filled with a golden, mystical light. It was definitely a higher, dimensional light. I had experienced this light one other time when I assisted a friend who had cancer die and leave this world. When she died, or passed through the dimensions into the Spirit world, the room filled with the same light. A multidimensional doorway had opened into the Spiritual realms. I was absolutely headed home. I was leaving my body and was beginning to move through this portal of light, home into the heavenly realm.

As I opened my eyes this morning, the whole room was filled with this same light. This light filled the whole bedroom, and I heard my mother speak to me in her very authoritative, know-it-all voice like she did when she was on the Earth. "Michelle, this is your mother, and I want you to listen to me!!!" I could also see my aunt Cecile whom I was very close to while she was on the Earth with her.

If things weren't bad enough, now my mother is with me. Again, she says, "Michelle, listen to me!!! It is not your time to go. If you leave the Earth now, your daughters and sister will not be able to get through this loss." (My mother and I weren't really close while she was on the Earth. She had a lot of issues with me, so I was surprised that she was here with me now, that she cared.)

She shows me my daughters' and sister's heartbreak in what they also are going through from the loss of Frank.

Then she says to me, "It wasn't your fault." All of a sudden, I had a memory of thinking Frank was sick as a child because of me. He had three kidney surgeries starting at six years old. His ureters had deteriorated, and they had to be reconstructed. When I was pregnant with Frank, I was 17 years old. I had my first period with him and didn't know I was pregnant. I was taking diet pills. Back in those days the doctors were prescribing Dexatrim, which is actually some kind of speed.

When he was first diagnosed with kidney problems, I felt like it was my fault, that taking the diet pills had caused it. I don't know if I ever shared that with anyone. The guilt was so painful, too much to think that I had caused my son to have the kidney problems.

Again, my mother said, "It wasn't your fault." The hidden guilt emotion surfaced, and I had the same experience that I had gone through the night before. I couldn't breathe. I felt like I was having a heart attack and my throat closed up. The hidden memory of my guilt was causing my heart to weaken, my lungs to freeze, and my throat to close up. As my mother continued to talk to me, the guilt started clearing, and I was able to start breathing again.

She takes me through my entire life with Frank, and the guilt that I felt for all of the times that I wasn't there for him.

Surfing was his life, and I never saw him surf. In his 20s he was on a baseball team, and I never saw him play because I was working in Sweden. My girls and friends used to go to his games. They had great fun. I missed out on much of his life and would give anything to have that time back with him, to be able to laugh and cheer him on. My sister and family were there, but I wasn't. I was on my spiritual tour … working.

My mother was showing me that Frank had a lot of love, laughter, and support. What I gave him was a foundation of love. Frank would tell me that he always knew I loved him, what a great mother I had been, always pushing us forward spiritually, looking for ways for us to heal. All I can feel now is I wish I had spent more time on the Earth with him.

My mother takes me through my whole life with Frank so I can let go of what I believed were my mistakes with him. The pain and grief started subsiding, clearing, and all I could feel was the love.

Next my mother takes me through our life together: first, letting me know how much she loved me. (I didn't feel it when she was alive.) I knew she must on some level, but I sure didn't feel it.

Starting with my birth, I remember when I was going to the holistic health college and became a rebirther, I was taken back in my birth experience, and I felt really confused. Later, I asked my mother if they gave her anything for her pain when I was born, and she said they gave her gas. That was my first experience of life on Earth: confusion. She also said that when I was born, it was the happiest day of her life. She had wanted a little girl so badly. I was absolutely shocked. I had always felt the opposite from her. Now she is showing me that moment again. I can feel the love from her. She then starts taking me through a tour of our life's journey together, all of our hurtful times and memories. She is doing Soul retrieval, bringing back into me, through my heart, all of the missing aspects of my self-love that were stuck in the hurtful memories.

As the love was filling my heart, the love energy was moving throughout my body into all of the places that were hurting: my back disk, my leg and foot that had weakened from meningitis many years ago. Soon my whole body was full of love and peace. I felt loved. My mother was showing me all of the people who loved me: my daughters, sister, my friend Judith. She wanted me to feel their love for me. She was showing me my brother's love and the love from the people whose lives I had touched while on the Earth and the importance of my spiritual journey and how much my spiritual mission and purpose woke our whole family up to the higher consciousness of God-Spirit.

When the process completed, I could still see and feel the whole room lit up. What a shocking surprise! My mother? As I write this, I feel a sense of completion with my mother, full circle, as the Creator writes about in the chapter that Frank loved so much.

My mother left this world in 2016, and I was grateful to be able to assist her through the birth canal back home into Spirit. I now felt like our journey was complete in some way. My mother left in love, and now for some reason she was assisting me to complete in love. As I write this, she is showing me that as a spiritual way shower, sometimes we sacrifice some of our own needs for the larger picture or purpose.

Today, after my healing experience with my mother, all I wanted to do was sleep. I had been through so much emotionally, and I was tired in mind, body and spirit.

Instead of spending time in Sweden's beautiful nature, I was inside sleeping. While I was sleeping, my mother was in my dream state watching over me. I can still feel her with me and feel her love and support. This is an interesting feeling experience and one I need to get used to. "Mom, you must be kidding."

On the Earth, she was one of the most unconscious people that I knew. She experienced life pretty much as black and white. She was raised in Unity Church, so she knew some of the principles but sure didn't practice them much. She was so afraid to die, which is why I wanted to be with her when she left this world. I wanted her to feel safe, which she did. But now, mom? As one of my guardian angels? "You must be kidding!"

May 19, 2018

I can't sleep and have been up since 3:30am. I slept all day yesterday. I thought maybe writing would help. I connected to Spirit, meditated, gave myself a healing and nothing is helping.

During my healing session for myself, I brought my inner children to me, both my inner little girl and boy.

My little girl said she is so lonely, which is the way I always felt as a child. It's not my adult who is lonely; it is the child aspect of myself. I never had a secure foundation, not from either parent, and now I am doing the same thing to myself, my inner little girl. I am traumatized and hurt because of memories that are surfacing of not being there for Frank and my children and yet I am not here for me. I need to love and nurture myself, the frightened child within me, and as I do, I will feel better, not so hurt, lonely and lost.

When I connected to my little boy, which is more physical, I could feel the physical pain in my heart. I was being shown that my body is very fragile, like glass ready to break and shatter. Because I have such a strong spiritual, light connection, I am not always aware of my physical body's imbalances or condition.

I was also being shown that Frank experienced the same thing. He was so connected to his light body, to his spiritual body, that he didn't really feel the weakness in his physical body.

May 20, 2018
Frank as my New Assistant

When I got up this morning, I was asking God for the strength to get through the day. I could not sleep again and have been up since 3:30am. I was going to start doing private sessions again today, but I wasn't even sure if I would be able to read people. I have so many people that want private sessions. My private sessions are always fully booked with a waiting list. Because I have had to cancel many of them, I am really backed up.

As I sat down to work with my first client, I closed my eyes to tune into the person's higher self, to receive information from Spirit about the person to be able to assist them to heal. I wasn't sure I would be able to make a clear connection. I was really surprised how easy it was to connect. The connection felt easier and stronger than it had ever been.

With Frank's passing, much of my own pain body has surfaced and cleared, and because of this my connection was pretty effortless. When I opened my eyes to talk to the person, I saw Frank sitting in the chair to the left. He was laughing, the laugh that I had heard so much while he was alive. He was laughing because he knew he was surprising me and that had been his intention.

He was with me all day and helped with all four of my sessions.

I felt very high energetically; being able to work with my son was so *incredible, amazing*. It was like nothing I could have ever imagined, and the helpful, extra energy from his assistance made the sessions much easier.

It was a good day. I felt elated until I got back to where I was staying. I felt him with me throughout the day and now I was once again alone. I walked through the door by myself and was very much alone. I wanted so badly for him to be in his physical body with me.

Many years ago, when I started my spiritual work, Jesus had taught me how to love, nurture and heal the child within myself. Our hurts, patterns, and belief systems are usually formed from our childhood. As we go back into the childhood and love, nurture, and validate the hurt child within ourselves, the adult starts feeling better. It is important to give our inner children everything that we needed but didn't receive.

Jesus had also shown me that we all have a little girl and boy. The little girl is our sensitivity, our feeling, our knowing – intuition, creative aspects of ourselves. Our little boy is the mental, the physical, the part that goes forward in life. Many times, these aspects of ourselves don't even know the other one exists. As we bring the little girl and boy together and validate them, they start feeling loved, safe and secure. As they start feeling loved, the adult us starts feeling safe to release old fears and self-worth issues. Through this release, the adult starts feeling loved, important, valuable, and balanced with our male/female aspects. This is the energy that we start putting out in the world and then bring back to us ... like attracts like.

We move out of the victim energy and take our power back from old hurts, patterns, and belief systems. As we gain a sense of self-worth and love, all of our relationships change, and we are able to move into gratitude and forgiveness.

CHAPTER EIGHT

The Review Room

May 21, 2018

I woke up after eight hours of sleep and had interesting dreams. In my dream, I was talking to my brother who had just returned from the holy land.

When I woke up from my dream, I could hear and feel my brother Tom praying over me; I could feel Tom with Jesus as he was praying for me. Through this grief healing process, I can feel that I have moved through many dimensions and timelines. I seem to be connecting with other people's energies and thoughts. I also heard and felt Frank saying, "Show me the way, Lord. Show me the way, Lord." He was reminding me to let go and let God.

I had private sessions today and was surprised at how much clearer I am in reading people's feelings and emotions: past, present and future — all together.

Much of my spiritual processes, my work with people, has been to assist them to release past trauma from this lifetime by following it back to other lifetimes to find the pattern or program that they have brought into this lifetime to heal. As we identify the pattern from another lifetime and release it, this frees the pattern in this lifetime. I (with Spirit) then do Soul retrieval and bring into the person the light, love, health, etc. that was trapped back in the other lifetimes. This is called Soul retrieval.

I have been shown that this is the lifetime we have agreed to come full circle, meaning this is a lifetime of completion. Nothing we go through is new. There is always a frame of reference someplace else, in another lifetime. Because there is really no past, present or future, we are living all of it now.

Past life regression is one of my specialties. It is not something I took classes to learn. My earliest conscious memory of living before was when I was about three years old. I have always known that I have lived many lifetimes before this one.

When I started assisting others with their own healing, people's past lives started surfacing, and I could see how the past lives were affecting this lifetime. With Spirit, I was shown how to clear and release them.

Now, in working with others, I can actually see and take people into their future consciousness on Earth. My spiritual team clears out their etheric bodies of karmic contracts, sicknesses, disease and then activates and opens the dimensions of the person's bodies for their future.

Spirit actually activates codings in the DNA systems of the new lifetime, the New Earth, that we are moving into multidimensionally.

It is very exciting for me to be able to assist people to clear their pain body, lower chakra energies. What a gift it is to be able to move into a new lifetime of joy and happiness, while on the Earth, to co-create Heaven on Earth.

Now, while working with people, Frank is always with me. He stands next to me on the left and puts his hand into people's thymus and pulls out old programming, patterns, sickness, disease, etc. As he pulls the old energy out, I can see it clearing from their whole body.

The Creator has shown me that the thymus is our new chakra for the new lifetime that we are collectively merging into. The color of this chakra is turquoise. Many times, when giving a person a healing session, they will say to me, "I see all of this turquoise energy around me." I haven't mentioned anything to them about the new chakra system. This is always such confirmation or validation from Spirit.

When I woke up this morning, Mother Mary was with me. Now I know why Jesus had brought Her to me in Bosnia; He knew Frank would be leaving and wanted His mother to be able to assist me through it.

Mother Mary certainly had the experience of losing a Son. She comforted me and shared Her love with me after Frank left. This morning, she was sharing something with me, but I was too tired, and I fell back to sleep.

When I woke up again this morning, I asked for Mother Mary to come and share the information with me again. I was so tired yesterday after the workshop that I couldn't remember much of what She had shared with me this morning.

Instead of Mother Mary coming, Frank and Jesus came. Jesus was supporting Frank in his new role with me. Frank was in white and his vibration was so high that he almost looked like a crystal portal.

The two of Them asked me to walk with Them, just as Jesus has done for so many years as he was teaching me my spiritual work.

This morning I was taken into a crystal room, like a temple with walls that were etheric. This is a room that people are taken into to review their life's experiences from the lifetime that they have just left behind. It is a review center. The center has many rooms; none have walls, but you don't hear another person's processes.

When people leave the Earth, they meet with loved ones on the other side for what could be called a reunion. Friends, relatives, or parents who they had not seen in a long time, are all there. There is a reunion and all people are happy in the higher picture of the lesson and come together in love and forgiveness.

How long a person stays in this energy is actually up to the person, or Soul. If one's earthly journey has been difficult, the Soul may want to stay in this love and Oneness for a while before they move on to the next process of reviewing their life.

The amount of time the Soul stays in this love and Oneness energy also depends on how evolved or conscious the Soul is. Some people, Souls, are very evolved and already understand that there is really nothing to forgive. They have worked on themselves, on family patterns, and already cleared what they had gone to the Earth to heal, learn and understand. These Souls may have been doing spiritual work, assisting others, and had moved spiritually back into love, gratitude and compassion for all. They already had a strong foundation of God, Christ, Love and faith in the highest of the religious belief from which they chose to learn.

When the person, Soul, feels it wants to move on, it is taken to the review temple to complete the earthly life that they have shifted out of.

In this room their entire life is shown to them as if watching a movie, beginning from the moment of conception, in the mother's womb and then their birth. What is different is the experience of the picture, the story that takes place from a higher perception, or understanding, of the lesson.

I was being taken through my life with Frank and saw all of my painful memories of the times that I wasn't with him or the things that I wish I had done differently. Although I have a spiritual understanding, after Frank left, I still felt so much hurt, pain and guilt for all of the times I wished I had been with him and chose to do other things instead. The loss has been very difficult emotionally. When I stay connected to him spiritually, in the higher dimensions, I feel light and free. When I move back down to the Earth plane, I once again experience the emotions of loss and grief.

In the review room, you actually experience and see your life as if you are reading a movie script. You review it from the choices you made for your life before you incarnated to the Earth. From the higher purpose you see why your Soul and the other Souls chose the experience. Some of it is hilarious because you already know what is going to happen. You wrote and designed the movie script before you came down to the Earth. Instead of living through the emotions of the movie, you review it from the lessons that you all agreed to go through and what you have learned from the agreements.

You experience the emotional growth that you and everyone in your play has gone through and what the lessons taught you.

You experience your life from the play, movie, or agreements instead of from the emotional pain and loss. You experience from your success in life, how much you grew, how much you understood, how much you learned, how much you were able to forgive and most of all, how much you loved – how much you were able to love and forgive others and if you were able to love and forgive yourself. How much meaning did your life give to others?

Sometimes other people's contracts, or agreements, affect us in the most challenging and difficult ways, but we agreed for them to be part of our movie or play for all of our Souls' growth and evolution.

As you go through the review, all of the painful emotions shift into love. They clear out of form and your emotional, etheric body becomes love, peace and gratitude. There is no such thing as a failure of your earthly lessons. You – we – are students and the Earth lessons are a class that we are going through. We design the movie to expand our Soul's knowledge and wisdom.

If you didn't understand or get a lesson in the class, you will come back to the Earth to take that part of the class again. There is no such thing as a failure; you might even laugh and say, "Oh, if only I had done it that way the outcome would have been better." You just sign up to take that part of the class again.

This would be like taking a math class and not understanding how to do math. You get a D or an F and just take the class again. In your review, you experience that it is not a big deal from you or Spirit.

It is actually the opposite. You feel grateful to be back in Spirit again and that you had the opportunity to participate in Earth's classes and to complete whatever your Soul needed to learn or experience.

There is much laughter and sharing in the review. I know everyone's review is different and there will be some painful, emotional, and sorrowful moments, but these moments will be transmuted into love once the higher understanding is experienced. Watching from a move script, all are actors who witness what kind of job they did in the role.

When my review was complete, all I could feel was love and freedom. When I came back into my earthly body and room, it took me a while to feel my body. I was very expanded and light. I could see my energy body full of colors. I was still vibrating in the crystal love, peace, and gratitude of the experience.

I didn't want to come back. I laid there for a long time and had to force myself to get up and write this down. It was fading out and I didn't want to lose the experience of what I was shown.

Frank's love for God and Jesus was not through a church or religion but from his higher connection to them from the Source. I had thought to myself many times that if he was to leave the Earth now, he would have left in the higher purpose of his Soul — what he had come to the Earth to learn.

Frank was love and saw the best in others. He worked at it. His intention was to experience life through the heart, love and wisdom of God and Jesus.

In my channeled books, workshops and lectures, the Creator has been sharing through me for about ten years that we are actually coming into a new lifetime without physically leaving the body. When the 2012 doorway opened, we collectively shifted, ascended into higher vibrations of ourselves multi-dimensionally.

When this doorway opened, many Souls started leaving the Earth back home into the Spirit world, and many others have shifted into a new lifetime without physically leaving the body.

We are in a death and rebirth cycle individually and collectively. As I mentioned, of the four books that I have written, the last one was Frank's favorite. The first chapter of "Death and Rebirth" was the one he loved. He read it over and over. He had two copies of the book in the hospital with him before he passed away. He gave one of the books to a nurse. He was excited that the nurse was very interested in it. He shared with me, "Just think, mom, as he heals himself (male nurse) his whole family unit will start healing." I smiled to myself. That is definitely my spiritual work and certainly Frank's intention.

As I said before, I believe that he left it for us to let us know that he knew he was leaving and wanted us to read that chapter as a gift to us, to remind us, to remember that we are in a death and rebirth cycle and that it was his time to go.

Frank took total responsibility for his life and physical conditions. He didn't blame anyone and saw the higher picture of his earthly journey. He had said to me that had he not gotten sick he would not have grown spiritually on the level that he had.

Frank loved other people and always saw the best in them. He wanted to help them and was very positive. He would not allow people to bring their negativity into his space. He would say it in love and always wanted people to see the highest and good in all situations.

Frank loved the Scalar Room Frequency Energy.* It really helped him. He even started growing his hair back from using scalar energy. He wanted to set his apartment up with Scalar Energy so people who didn't have money would be able to use it for free.

May 30, 2018
Wings of Love

It has been 46 days since Frank left this world. The last days have been such a blur. So many days ago, and yet is seems like yesterday. Many people have sent love blessings and condolences. I could truly feel everyone's love and support. The collective love and support have been like wings of love that have held me up, held me together to be able to move through this.

I know I could not have gotten through this alone. Thought is energy and I could feel people's prayers holding me in the heart of God, of Love, of some sort of safety net and hope.

---

* Scalar Room Frequency Energy: The Scalar Wave Field Room offers times of escape from this electronic "pollution" and allows for a recharge of your body & a rejuvenation of your cells. Just like getting out of the city and going to the country or the mountains to take a big breath of fresh, clean air not only is good for you but feels good as well. Time spent in this Scalar Wave Field is that "breath of fresh air" for your cells' energy.

CHAPTER NINE

Frank's Earthly Birthday

June 2, 2018

My Swedish friend, Judith, knew Frank and she agreed to spend his birthday with me. One of Judith's favorite sacred healing spots is an old Viking grave. She had spent many hours there. While Frank was living in Sweden for a few months, he had gone to this place with Judith. We decided to spend part of Frank's birthday at the Viking power spot.

As I started walking the path to the grave's power spot, Mother Mary appeared next to me on my right. I felt at peace with Her. Her motherly love filled my whole body and Being with love, light and a presence of harmony, like everything was in perfect order, as it should be.

I felt as if She were my mother, loving and nurturing me and also a mother of a son. Once again, I felt our hearts become One heart and my whole Being vibrated in silence and perfection like I was home. No words needed to be exchanged.

I looked up and saw Jesus and Frank walking in front of us. We were all walking in the light of love, peace and perfection.

Somehow, I knew that Frank's whole journey had led to this birthday, the rebirth of himself into the Spirit world.

His intention on Earth was to help and assist others who were having difficult challenges in life. Now as the Master Healer that he is in higher dimensions, he can reach and help many people.

Today was a good day.

June 3, 2018

How could Frank's birthday be such a high, good day and this one be so challenging? I saw some of the things that my daughter posted on Facebook about Frank and his birthday, and my emotional loss of my son felt like we were both at the beginning again. I cried and sobbed at the loss of my beautiful son not being on the Earth with me. I would never hear his voice calling to say "Hi, mom. I just called to tell you I love you."

All of the memories of his hospital stay and how he died came up for me again.

From the other side, Frank is telling me not to go there, to stay connected to him in his new lifetime in Spirit. As long as I am there, I am okay. It's when my mind takes me back to him leaving that the pain is too unbearable. He died two times. Although I am very grateful that I had those days with him in the hospital before he left this world, the pain of knowing that he was so excited to have a second chance at life and that he was really going for it was excruciating. God had given him a chance that many people don't get and then he was gone. The higher aspect of me knew that it was his time to go, but the human me was feeling challenged.

I decided for now I cannot listen or watch my daughter's posts. It takes me back into the middle of the loss, like a dark hole with no way out.

I have felt it is very important to grieve, which I certainly have done and will continue to do when it comes up spontaneously and when I feel the built-up emotion that needs releasing. But I also want to honor Frank and stay connected to him in his new home and higher state of consciousness

This process is not denial; it is a rewiring of my brain from my lower chakra pain body of grief and loss, of karmic choices, to my higher chakra, heart of God's Love system.

I was talking to Judith about all of this and what a hard time Jennifer is having moving through the loss. At that time my phone that is plugged in across the room starts ringing.

When I walk over to answer it, I could see that Jennifer is calling me. It rang several times and I kept trying to answer it, but I could not open the phone up to answer the call.

I called her right back a couple of times, and she wasn't answering the call. The next morning, I looked to see who called and there was no call from her. When I talked to her later that day, she said she hadn't called me.

Frank was at it again! I could hear him laughing in Spirit.

CHAPTER TEN

Stockholm Workshop with Frank

June 2018

While I was setting up for the workshop, Frank immediately dropped into the room. I call it dropping in because that is what the experience feels like. It feels like a spiritual doorway between Heaven and Earth opens and Frank comes into the room through the doorway.

Other people also experience him dropping into the room.

Frank was talking and laughing with me the whole time. He was excited about assisting me with this workshop. His presence was with us the whole two days. I even put a chair next to mine in front of the room for him to sit next to me as my assistant during the workshop.

In the beginning of the workshop, a woman came up to me and handed me angel wings. She did not know that Frank had passed. She pointed up above and said, "I don't know why, but someone up above told me to bring these to you."

Frank was standing on the right side of me and started laughing. We call him Angel Frank. Angel Frank was at it again. He wanted me to know that he was still very much with me, maybe not physically, but very much spiritually.

When he is connecting to me personally, he is always on the right. When he is working with the group or in my private sessions, he is always on my left.

He was a very powerful assistant, and through him, the higher Spiritual realms were wide open for all of us.

During and after the healing processes that I would take people through, Frank was right there, talking, encouraging and laughing with people.

While in a process, one of the women was having a hard time letting go of old emotions, and Frank put his hand into her heart and thymus and pulled the old, fear energies out of her. Her heart opened up to feel love and peace.

Another woman who is an artist also had a very powerful healing experience with Frank. He cleared her heart, thymus and body out of old, frozen energy. As this was happening, she felt herself shift multidimensionally in the higher, Spiritual realms.

The shift opened her up through Heaven's doorways and into all of the beautiful music and colors of the higher realms. While she was floating in these realms, her whole system experienced an upgrade, out of third dimension and into the Oneness. She said she could hardly wait to go home and paint the new colors and her new experiences of the Spiritual world.

Many other miracles and healings were taking place for the whole group.

We were all experiencing ourselves vibrating together beyond our earthly veils and into our higher selves' energy.

I could still feel my mother's energy with me, in my spine and nervous system. She had stayed with me and had been very much present with me since she intervened to stop me from leaving this world when she told me it was not my time to leave.

When I took the group into the Mother's ancestral DNA systems, I felt my mother release the hold that she had on me. I felt free, like myself again. My mother's energy was very different than mine, and I was having a hard time with the grip that she had on me. I wanted to be in my own energy again.

At that moment, I realized that she had stayed with me to keep me in my body. She was concerned that I may slip out of my body back into the Spiritual world.

At that time, I had a vision of when I was young with my children. We didn't have and use seat belts. While driving, if I came to a stop or was slowing down, I would always put my arm out across the front seat so my child would not fly forward and end up hurt. This vision was humorous. I could see my mother stretching her arm out across me so I wouldn't fly forward and out of my body, into the Spiritual world.

Her intention was absolutely to keep me in my body, and that she did.*

Once again, this workshop was the highest that had ever come through me. We were definitely One with the Spiritual world.

Frank continues to open the door to the Spiritual world for all of us. Thank you, Frank, and thank all of you amazing Beings of light from the Spiritual world that are assisting us through the Ascension doorways to co-create Heaven on Earth.

*This was the beginning of an incredible healing journey that I would go through with my mother. She would heal our relationship, her relationship with me, from the Spiritual world.

June 19, 2018
Easy Peasy

I am completing my Sweden tour and getting ready to go back to Hawaii to assist to put Frank's affairs in order. My assistant, Mia, is dropping me off at the place where I am staying in Stockholm. I thank her for all of her love, support and assistance while I have been in Stockholm. She responds, "Easy peasy!" I asked her, "What did you say?" She looks surprised, kind of blank and says, "I don't know." I tell her she has just said easy peasy and ask her if that is something she usually says. Again, she looks blank, surprised and says no.

Easy peasy was one of Frank's expressions that he used often. It meant to him that, yes, it is easy — no problem.

I had to laugh and felt joy. I knew once again that Frank was with me and had sent that thought to Mia. I have experienced others using that term with me and like Mia, it is not a term that they use.

Frank is always letting me, his sisters, his daughter, Monica and others know that he is very much with us. He is always sending signs to us.

CHAPTER ELEVEN

My Return to Hawaii

June 21, 2018

I am back in Hawaii to assist in cleaning out Frank's apartment, so Monica can rent it, sell it or whatever she decides to do with it.

When Frank was first diagnosed with being sick, I pleaded with him to fill out a will. I even brought the papers to him. I know in his mind that he thought making out a will would be putting his energy into dying, and he very much wanted to live.

While he was in the hospital after his death experience, we had talked about him making out a will, and he was very much wanting to do that, but he passed away before that could happen.

Frank did not leave a will or any instructions, but I knew he wanted to leave his apartment to his daughter, Danilla. His apartment was paid off and was free and clear. He had mentioned to me many times that if anything happened to him that his apartment was financial security for her future.

This is a very difficult and heartbreaking experience. I feel like I am going through his death again, letting go again. My mind has an understanding of the process, like layers of an onion, peeling off layer by layer, but my heart feels the depth of the loss, like a bottomless pit of pain and grief.

When I walked into his apartment the other night, my whole body went into grief mode; if there is such a thing as a grief mode, I experienced it. I felt my body tighten up, and I had a hard time breathing like I had the first day of that first phone call from my daughter, Jennifer, letting me know of Frank's condition. I felt the same fear and was shaking inside.

The next day, I had no energy. I could not force myself to get up, get dressed or even function. I needed to make some phone calls to find a probate attorney and to contact the person who was completing the video of Frank's celebration of life, but I could not do it.

I felt so much fear, the same fear that was activated when I went into his apartment. The fear had such a gripping effect. I absolutely could not pick up the phone to have a conversation with anybody and certainly not to ask questions about my son's death.

I thought if I meditated, the fear would subside, but it didn't. Nothing seemed to help. I sobbed knowing that I would never see my beautiful son on the Earth again. I would not hear his voice or his message: "Hi mom. This is Frank. I just called to tell you that I love you!"

I felt split, guilty. I have such a great connection to him in Spirit, but he is gone from the Earth with me. The Spirit world has always been very easy for me to live in. The Earth plane has been the challenge.

I have always known that God is my real parents. As a little girl, I used to cry myself to sleep at night because I wanted to be home with my real mommy and daddy. I used to cry, "Mommy, daddy, please let me come home." I felt like I was being punished because I had to be down on the Earth.

While in India in 2004, I went through a near death experience (NDE) and I didn't want to come back to the Earth. Jesus and my team told me that it wasn't my time to come home. I still had work to do with others on the Earth, to assist them into higher knowledge, understanding of themselves and the Spirit world. I didn't want to return to the Earth, but when I did, I felt like I had just woken up. I experienced the Earth and its beauty for the first time in a higher frequency. Spirit and I had become one on the Earth; we had integrated.

Before the near-death experience, I was channeling Spirit, but now Spirit was living and breathing through me, through my spiritual teachings and purpose in a new wholeness.

With Frank's departure from the Earth, I again felt like I wanted to be home in the Spirit world. Spirit is such an easy place to be; the Earth is the challenge.

My guilt was coming from knowing that people are doing everything possible to have access to the Spirit world, and I have always had it and Frank is with me, communicating with me daily. I am having a hard time being without him on the Earth. I know he did not die; he has just changed addresses and I talk to him daily but not on the Earth.

In between my sobbing, Frank, Jesus and my team came to me and took me once again into the golden field. The golden field seems to be the meeting place for us to connect the Spiritual world with our human earthly world.

Because there is no past, present or future, they took me into the future of my life with Frank's daughter, Danilla. I watched her graduate from high school and felt how proud we all were of her and what a beautiful, healthy young woman she had become. Frank was so proud of her. I was then shown her graduation from college and then fast forwarded to her as a mother to a beautiful, little girl.

I experienced Frank watching over her as she continued to mature through her earthly life. He really was and is an amazing guardian angel of hers. I witnessed that he never feared for her after his earthly death because he had access to the future and knew that she would have a beautiful life. He also knew that Monica, Danilla's mother, would give her a great, safe foundation.

This is not to say that she would not go through any of the lessons that her Soul had signed up to go through. The first difficult lesson was the loss of her father at barely 12 years old. The loss impacted her life and choices in so many ways.

As I watched Danilla mother her beautiful, little girl, I could see that she was giving her child the same kind of foundation that Frank had given her when she was a child.

I was also shown that her little girl was an aspect of her mother's mother, her grandmother from the other side of the family, her mother's family. She passed from this world before Danilla was born.

After being shown the future of Danilla's life, I fell fast asleep for about two hours.

Since returning to Hawaii, I was once again having a hard time sleeping and was very grateful to be able to sleep.

When I woke up, I still felt the paralyzing fear and was not able to reach out to anyone regarding Frank. That evening, I was telling my sister about the fear that I had felt and experienced so much in my life.

I felt like I should have been working on the book but didn't have any energy to function and could not even tune into what I needed to write about.

While in the fear, I even thought that perhaps I was crazy to think that we were going to write a book together. About what? Death – rebirth - Spirit world? Who cares? There is so much being written. What new insight do I have to offer?

As I was going to bed that night, the clock read 12:12. Okay, Frank. I know you are once again communicating and letting me know you are with me. More and more number sequences were coming through from Frank.

June 22, 2018

As I awoke this morning, I woke up with what I call the holy light coming into me. This time the beam of light was coming into my heart, and all I could feel was overwhelming love filtering and expanding through my entire body.

Mother Mary was once again with me, and I could feel her love and compassion for me. As the light continued to fill the room with love, I saw my inner little girl and boy come towards me. While in Sweden, they were so afraid and alone. I had reconnected with them and promised them that they were safe and that we would get through this together, but I forgot to stay connected.

Grief is such a frozen energy that the highest intentions seem to get lost in the middle of the pain and sorrow.

I had taught Inner Child Healing many years ago in my private sessions and workshops. Now, in sessions and workshops, I always introduce people to their inner children. Many times, people don't even know that they exist.

I have an understanding of the pain, fear, grief, loss and lack of safety that our inner children feel, but I forgot to reconnect with mine.

When I was in Sweden, one of the major things that assisted me to start shifting through the pain was to nurture my inner children. When they started feeling safe so did I, the adult. Now I was once again in the old, frozen fear that had consumed much of my life.

As I brought them to me, I started reassuring them that they, we, were safe, that we are with our real parents now, Mother/Father/God/Creator, and that we can talk to Frank any time we want. He did not die; he is very much alive, just not with us on the Earth anymore. This reassurance started clearing some of the fear that I had been experiencing.

As I talked to, loved and reassured my inner children, my little girl and boy, of their safety, my subconscious opened up to an old memory of fear.

The Creator talks about the subconscious being like Google. Every experience our Soul has ever gone through is in our subconscious mind. When we go through an emotional experience in this lifetime or other lifetimes, the subconscious will open up and download the similar emotional experience. Because there is really no past, present or future, we experience all of the emotions at once. Not only the painful memories but the same is true for positive memories. However, the painful memories are the ones with the hardest, or deepest, impacts.

As I was holding my little girl and boy, I was taken back to a memory when I was five years old. I still remember it vividly. I don't remember waking up but do remember walking down the stairs to my mother's screams. As I stood in the middle of the stairs, I looked over and saw my father with his hands around my mother's neck, choking her to death. He was drunk, and when he saw me, he stopped. My mother and I locked eyes, and we both knew at that instant that I had saved her life. We were definitely Soul to Soul. In a very frightened voice she said, "It's okay, honey. Just get a drink of water."

I don't remember the next day, but all four of us kids were put into a foster home. The family that took us kept us all together. I was absolutely terrified, no safety. Was my mother dead or alive? No one explained anything to us.

I had an older brother, Mike, who was 8 years old, a younger sister, Melody, who was 4 years old, and a 2 ½ year old brother, Tommy. The people who took us in were very mean to us, and I was always afraid, concerned, and heartbroken over the way they treated us and my little brother, Tommy.

The three of us older kids slept in an attic room together. I was terrified most of the time and was always afraid that someone was in the room with us.

The foster parents were very religious, and we went to church with them constantly. They belonged to the Assembly of God Church. They had two daughters about the same age of my sister and I, four and five. If their girls ever had disagreements with us, they always won, and we were punished. As I said, they were very religious, and we went to church with them three times a week. The father of the family was a devout prayerful man, and at the same time, he was also sexually molesting me. Because of my childhood and the sexual molestation, I grew up with no inner boundaries. I felt worthless, not important or valuable enough to keep safe. I didn't even know that I could say no; I was lost.

My self-worth had been shattered.

I find it interesting that when I am speaking to a group, I will ask if anyone in the audience has ever had any self-worth issues, and almost everyone raises their hands.

This is the lifetime that we have agreed to come to the Earth to experience self-love, the love and safety that we experience when we are home in the Spirit world.

As a healer, I have looked at this story many times and thought I had pretty much let go of it emotionally, but what I experienced now was that the loss of Frank triggered the fear of my mother being dead and I went into the paralyzing fear that my inner children used to feel. There was no safety and no one to reach out to, to keep us or me safe.

Our childhood was a nightmare. My father had been in the South Pacific during WWII and was in the front lines. He was a big man, and because of his size, he carried a big gun (a BAR — Browning Automatic Rifle). My parents met the night he returned from WWII.

In those days, no one knew about PTSD, which he had. We moved every year, sometimes twice a year; sometimes

I went to two schools in one year.

My father being drunk, beating up my mother, and flipping out was pretty much a normal experience. Afterwards, he would feel guilty and take off somewhere. He would then want to start over and would bring us, his family, with him for a new beginning. We had one or two new beginnings every year.

I don't know how long we were in the foster home, maybe a year. My parents got back together for another new beginning.

This morning, as I was holding my inner children and reassuring them that they were safe, my subconscious had googled up my foster home memories. While holding and loving the child within me, my fear started to subside. In fact, the paralyzing fear that I would have to push through in much of my life had subsided. I actually felt joyful and free, and my energy had returned.

As long as I have been doing spiritual work, I am still amazed at the access we have within us to heal and how our brain compartmentalizes fear memories to keep us safe until the time is right to let go of the painful experiences.

For the moment, another new beginning: I absolutely know that my foster home story is now past history.

The Creator talks about this being the lifetime we have agreed to come full circle. Nothing new has happened to us in this lifetime. Everything that we have ever gone through and are now going through has a frame of reference someplace else, other lifetimes and other patterns.

The patterns that we are clearing in this lifetime run through our Soul's history, through our Akashic Records. We are here to move through many karmic agreements and back into the Oneness without physically leaving our bodies – coming home within ourselves. Our healing process is like peeling an onion, through the tears we move into the core or center of our own self-love, self-worth and acceptance.

CHAPTER TWELVE

My Return to Sedona

Late June 2018

After I returned to Sedona, I reached out to and had a reading by an incredible psychic channel by the name of Mary Allison. She said her specialty was not bringing loved ones through from the other side, but she would see what she could do.

Although I was already communicating with Frank, I wanted confirmation from someone else.

Frank immediately appeared and was anxious to share information with us. Of course, the first thing that he shared was that it was his time to go.

He said that after the operation he did not know that he had died. He was down at the beach and someone named Nancy, another spirit, told him that he was no longer in his body, that he had died. He immediately went back to the hospital and was with us the whole time we were in his hospital room with his body.

The reason we felt like he was just asleep and would wake up any minute is because he was in the room with us the whole time and still very connected to his body. This is why his body was still warm. He said he wanted us to remember him like that, like he was still alive because he was and is. He is no longer in a physical form but still very much alive, more alive than when he was in his body.

He then shared that after his body was taken back downstairs, doctors were doing something to his body trying to figure out what went wrong, like an autopsy, but the hospital never shared this with us.

Then Frank started talking about a woman whom he loved very much. He kept repeating, "She is so beautiful." I said, "I think that is his daughter that he is talking about." Every time I would talk to him on the phone, he would always talk about how beautiful Danilla was.

Mary Allison asked me what she looks like and when I told her, she said, "Yes. It is definitely his daughter."

Frank also shared what we, the family and I, believed: that he had come back to the Earth for a few days to be able to complete with everyone in love and for everyone to be able to complete with him in love. As I mentioned, while in the hospital, he told his father that he loved him. Those were his last words that they shared with each other.

Monica, Frank's ex-wife, was also able to let go of her emotions from the divorce and come back to love.

As I mentioned before, Frank definitely left this world in love, love from everybody and love for everybody.

Never in my life did I feel I could ever express gratitude in any way or that there was any gift in Frank leaving this world.

When he left, my heart shattered, I was broken open. As I started releasing my pain and grief, I started experiencing that I actually had more room to feel love for others. My heart is very much open to have love and compassion for other people's lives and journeys.

I am able to experience a new expanded level of love that I had no idea even existed. I had always felt love and compassion for others, but now there is no filter. I see and experience the world and all of us here through the heart of Christ Love and caring, through a higher lens of perception.

I am very grateful that my heart and mind are the heart and mind of God. I am also grateful that my son is still very much with me and is my constant assistant in my spiritual work.

Frank also shared that we will continue to feel him with us and around us. He will continue to communicate to us through numbers and other signs. He is actually quite humorous in his communications. For months after he left, I would always see the numbers that he was communicating to us. 11-11, the numbers that he gave to Danilla the night that he left this world. 11-11, 12-12, 444, and 333 seem to be his favorites.

12-12 connects you to the golden light of Christ energy, which will awaken divine love within you and activate new energies and frequencies. 12-12 is the number to help you evolve through the ascension into higher dimensions of yourself and into the consciousness of the new Earth.

Frank Making Contact with Family

Frank Connecting with Monica and Danilla

Since my mom passed on 12/11/01, she always comes to say hello or comfort me with an 11:11. Sometimes, it's with a 22:11 or an 11:22, since she was born on 11/22/39.

Frank and I both always looked at the TV digital clock, and if an 11:11 would pop, he would say, "Ciao, Cecilia!" to my mom.

The night Frank passed away, I remember driving home from the hospital under the loudest thunderstorm ever. The sky was covered with lightning. I remember thinking that it must be Frank; he was not happy to leave Danilla ....

Once at home, I gave the sad news to Danilla. We both finally laid down in bed to go to sleep at about 1:30 am. I asked Danilla if she wanted her dad to speak to her through the numbers. As she said yes, my iPhone that was plugged to charge right there in the bedroom, lit up, illuminating the room. As I immediately leaned to looked at it, I saw the time: 11:11! Danilla said hello to her Dad.

One night I woke up to a dream: I was in my home in Italy, and I walked out to the bedroom's hallway. It was dark, and I could not see anything, but I could feel Frank next to me, and sense his breathing. I woke up and jumped off the bed and stared at the phone ... it showed 3:39. Since then, the number 33 keeps on appearing to us, and we started to connect it to Frank.

It can be a silly thing Danilla says or does: a rainbow we see, a special moment we share, when the number 33 will pop up somewhere around us.

Months later, I had a vision in my dream. Frank was beautiful and young, just like when we got married. He was tan and healthy, and he was smiling at me. I could only see his arm and torso, and he was not wearing a t-shirt. White, sheer drapes were coming down from above and surrounding him. It was such a beautiful, serene and peaceful moment.

Jennifer's Musings about Frank

Before Frank passed away, Danilla and I were walking down a street in Waikiki. We were walking past the Victoria's Secret store. Alongside the high-rise building, there's a huge Victoria's Secret billboard. As we were walking by, Danilla laughs, and says, "Every time we walk by this, my dad always looks up and says, 'Hey, Ladies! How's it going?'" After Frank passed away, my mom, my sister, my aunty and I were sitting in his apartment, all sad, and going through his things. I look up and I see this little, pink Victoria's Secret bag. I thought it was odd, and I asked, "What's in the Victoria's Secret bag?" My auntie said, "Oh, it's the weirdest thing; that's the bag the mortuary put Frank's ashes in to give to me." I was like, "Oh my God! No way! Then I told them the story about how Danilla and I were walking down Waikiki, and how she said her dad always used to say 'Hello, ladies,' like flirting with the Victoria's Secret billboard. It would totally be my brother's sense of humor to have his ashes sent home in a Victoria's Secret bag.

My brother was Mr. Positive. If you started to be negative, he'd cut you off (which used to irritate me so badly), and he'd say, "How about those Mets?" A couple of weeks after Frank passed away, I started seeing numbers: usually the number 4 and the number 3 in different sequences. One night, I was texting with my girlfriend, and I was telling her how I keep seeing certain numbers over and over. She texted me back a screenshot, and it was of her clock: 11:44 p.m. at night. She said, "Hmm, I wonder what this means." I just dismissed it and thought, "I don't know." The next day I was at work and was upset about my ex-boyfriend. I had all of these negative thoughts spinning around in my head about him, when all the sudden, my phone dropped on the floor and lit up. When I went to grab it, it was 11:44 a.m. Now, that struck me as odd because I remembered the screen shot my girlfriend sent asking what 11:44 meant, so I decided to Google it. It stated that 11:44 is your angels sending you a message to keep your thoughts positive. I was so blown away, and I knew that it was my brother telling me to stop being so negative. After that, I would randomly see the numbers 11:44; it seemed like I saw them everywhere I went. I walk into the store thinking negative thoughts, and there in big writing is the price: the low price of $11.44 - right as I was thinking negatively - my brother's way of reminding me to stop being negative.

My brother had a great sense of humor. He would sing songs and add his own words to them. A song that he would always sing to me and put my name into the lyrics was "Don't worry. Be Happy." He'd sing, "Jen. No worries. Be happy!" A couple of months after my brother passed away, I was having a bad day. My sons and I were driving down the road in Frank's truck, a road that I've driven down a thousand times, and all of the sudden, I look up and on the telephone pole was a hand-painted sign that I'd never seen before that somebody had just put up. It read: No Worry. Be Happy. I was like, "OMG! Did you guys see that?" I drive this road every day and have never seen that sign. I had to turn around and take a picture of it.

There are a lot of songs that remind me of my brother, particularly any of U2's older songs and Talking Heads' songs. I have my brother's truck, and it's the darndest thing. I never hear Talking Heads or old U2 songs on the radio, and there were a few months that it seemed every time I'd get into his truck, I'd turn the radio on and either U2 or Talking Heads would be playing. Sometimes, I'd be in a negative head space or just needed a reminder to connect spiritually, and boom! I'd get in his truck, and U2 or Talking Heads would be playing on the radio. I'd just giggle out loud and say, "Thanks, big bro. I needed that reminder." One time, I got in his truck thinking how awesome it is that he always somehow arranges that to happen. I start his truck up, get started down the road, and I say, "So, what you got for me today, big bro?" kind of joking like wondering which song he was going to play. Then, I turn on the radio, and it's a new U2 song playing … one that I've never heard before called "Get out of your own way."

> Get out of your own way
> Get out of your way, oh, I could sing it to you all night
> If I could, I'd make it all right.
> Nothing's stopping you except what's inside
> I can help you, but it's your fight, your fight
> Get out of your own way
> Get out of your own way

I was so shocked! I couldn't believe it; the song was so fitting. I had a permanent grin from ear-to-ear. I remember crying tears of Joy thinking of how incredible my connection to my big brother is.

On the one-year anniversary of my brother's transition, my girlfriend and I went for a drive. I brought all my Angel cards, and we sat down at a restaurant to have a glass of wine, do Angel readings, and have a toast to our Angel Frank. We sat there for a while reading the profound messages we were receiving from our cards. We had just made a toast, and I said to my big brother, "Thank you so much for everything you agreed to go through and all the amazing lessons you've been teaching me. Cheers, big bro! I love you so much." (which happens to be pretty much the last thing I said to him, like hours before he passed) when all of the sudden, the Earth started shaking. Everything in the restaurant started swaying. We were having a huge earthquake! We grabbed our things and ran outside. After it was over, I realized that it was close to the time that Frank had made his transition a year earlier. I called my aunty who was on Oahu with my sister-in-law, my niece and some friends celebrating Frank's one year as an Angel. I was so excited. I called her and said, "Aunty, we just had the biggest earthquake! What time did Frank pass away?" It turned out that the Earth shook at the same time as my brother's time of death a year earlier. It was so crazy and really unbelievable. I was dumbfounded. Nowadays, what I know - what he's taught me - is that everything's possible, so I acknowledge all the connections. I acknowledge all the messages, and I live from a place of gratitude.

I miss him all day, every day, and wish he was here physically to touch, to hug, to hear him play guitar, to hear his jokes, to get irritated at his "How about those Mets?" comment. But what I do have is a connection that's always on. I feel like I know him, and I am connected to him in a way that I never was before. I feel protected and guided by my big bro in a way that is beyond what our humanness can comprehend. My brother has taught me that, really, there's no such thing as death. Death is a human concept that we've made up to try and reason why our physical body leaves. But I take comfort in what Frank's taught me - that he lives on - even more so than before.

These are just a few of my daily experiences.

Frank Connecting with his Sister Tricia

Frank connects with Tricia through the numbers 11:11, 1:11, 333, 222, and he always make sure the buzzer on her dryer goes off, even though Tricia makes sure it is turned off. Frank seems to think this is pretty funny, and he certainly gets Tricia's attention.

444 are the angel numbers, and 333 and 13 are the Christ numbers. I believe 11-11 is a master number that combines the angels and masters energetically. They are collectively continuing to open the doors for us to awaken into the higher purpose of our assignment here on Earth. They also have opened a doorway of light for us to remember that we are a divine aspect of the Creator in human form. We are awakening into our own inner master and co-creator; it is important to remember that we have chosen this lifetime. It is important for us to be conscious of our thoughts and what energetically we are putting out to the world, because our thoughts create our reality.

Both of my daughters constantly see the number 1-11. This is a very high number reminding them to stay positive, which Frank always was. It is a number of new beginnings and a reminder to watch your thoughts because they create your reality. My daughter, Tricia, sees 222, which means you are being guided by Spirit, hidden love and power, and is symbolic of unity.

My phone is full of snapshots of the dates and numbers being downloaded to me from Frank.

The reason our loved ones on the other side can communicate with us through numbers is because all dimensions have computer systems. I have been shown and experienced these systems while visiting the Spirit world.

The computer systems in the higher dimensions are crystalline. Our systems have crystal in them but are not the higher frequencies of those in the higher dimensions. Our loved ones are able to send numbers to us from these systems.

I was also told that our computer technology was downloaded to us from the higher dimensions.

September 2018
Sallee Experiencing Frank's Love and Support

This was a challenging time in my life — a time when I questioned and struggled with being on the Earth.

I was now living in the Phoenix, AZ area and had come north to Sedona for a day or two. I went to Red Rock Crossing to sit by the water, to connect and ground to the Earth. I was sitting there on a rock looking around when I suddenly had the awareness that Frank was with me. As I looked out at the trees, the water and Cathedral Rock, I was seeing it all very differently. I was looking through his eyes. The trees were so full of life. Everything was so alive, and my Spirit was lifted and renewed.

I felt like myself again, alive and "in love" with life! I was out of the story and back in harmony with my Truth and Light. I felt like Love. I cried with tears of joy and thanked Frank for the experience, this gift.

CHAPTER THIRTEEN

Mother Mary Healing Me

July 31, 2018

This morning I woke up in grief, in pain and crying over the loss of Frank. I was also sick. After being gone for four months when I returned home to Sedona, I collapsed. I was exhausted, mentally, emotionally and physically. I literally could not get out of bed, which added to the emotional pain that I was experiencing.

I had been sick a lot in this lifetime. For years I had a very weak immune system and when I traveled on airplanes, was in airports or train stations, around a lot of people, I would usually end up sick.

However, the last couple of years I have felt very strong and have not been sick at all! I was surprised that even going through everything with Frank that I did not get sick.

And now here I am back in Sedona, and I can't get out of bed. I can't remember being this sick, but I don't think I will die from it because my mother had told me a few months ago that it wasn't my time to go. I realize I am letting go of everything.

As I lay there crying, I asked Spirit for help, and Mother Mary came to wrap me in the Mother's love, reminding me of the larger picture of what She had shown me at the pyramids. She had shown me the larger picture of Her agreement with the Creator and Jesus.

She then took me into the larger picture of my agreement with the Creator and Frank.

First, she wrapped Her energy around me as a cloak of love so

I would feel safe and nurtured in a Mother's love - the love that I did not receive from my mother in this lifetime.

She then took me back into my mother's womb when she was pregnant with me. My mother smoked over a pack of cigarettes a day. I was shown how the cigarettes had affected my immune system. This would be like a little baby smoking over a pack of cigarettes a day. I am a sensitive, and this really affected the growth and strength of my immune system. This was before women knew how bad smoking would be on a child's health. It was before people were aware of how cancer and other diseases were connected to cigarette smoking.

Mother Mary started clearing the memories and toxicity out of my etheric DNA systems and out of my cells and tissues.

After She cleared me, Jesus came, and together They took me to the golden fields to meet Frank again.

I knew this Being standing there was my son, but he had expanded so much multidimensionally that is was a bit challenging for me.

As I stood there many memories of our life together started coming up like a reel of film. These were all of our magical times together. I could feel the love, the joy, humor and the support that we had been for each other. During the difficult experiences in my life, Frank was there for me. He was my cheerleader, telling me what a great mother I had been, that I was always looking for ways for us to heal and grow and that I was always pulling us through everything.

I really needed to feel and remember this now because once again I was going into my pain of all the times I wasn't there for him and my children.

He then showed me how my DNA system had led him to the beautiful light conscious, loving man that he was when he left this world. As my DNA unraveled into my higher DNA of God,

Spirit, Love, forgiveness and gratitude, his DNA shifted into these frequencies.

He reminded me that we still have the same DNA and now that he is expanding into his higher multidimensional selves and purpose, he is pulling all of us with his earthly DNA into these higher dimensions of awakening also.

I know this to be true because all of us, his sisters, myself, his ex-wife and my family have definitely moved into a higher meaning, a higher purpose of what is important in life. It feels like veils have been lifted, and many old imbalances have dissolved. All of us including many of his friends have definitely shifted our perceptions of life beyond judgements, etc. and into love, into seeing all in its perfection and that all is being played out exactly as it should.

I certainly feel this with Frank. When I connect to him on the other side, I feel love, harmony, grace, how everything is in perfection.

Then I will hear a song, see a child or someone will say something, and I will be back into my earthly grief and loss of my son. But, I am definitely starting to feel there is a light at the end of this darkness.

After the healing and connection with Mother Mary, Jesus and Frank, I was able to get up, fix some tea and actually write this experience down.

August 2, 2018

Today was a hard day. I cried and cried missing Frank so much. He was with me in Spirit and telling me to lay down and call him just like he used to call me on the phone when he was on the Earth. I can call him in Spirit.

As I laid down, I felt the holy light come into me. I called on

Frank, Peter, Jesus, Mother Mary, Magdalene, Archangel Michael and my whole team. I felt my whole body start melting into peace, love and harmony. I could feel Frank with me. He was talking to me about my future on the Earth and that the best of life was yet to come for me.

My whole life has been of service to God - Spirit and like many of you, I have gone through many challenges on Earth or what Spirit calls karmic completions.

Losing Frank has been the hardest for me. Frank was telling me and showing me that the hard, karmic part of my life was over, that I had shifted into a new lifetime on Earth without physically leaving the body. He was showing me what my life was going to be like.

I felt the love, support and gratitude from my whole spiritual team.

I had felt guilty lately when I prayed for myself because I see so many in the world whose lives are so much more difficult than mine.

Yes, my son left this world, but I still connect with him on the other side. I still have and love my girls. My health is much to be grateful for. I work in Sweden and have seen some of the refugees coming into the country that have lost everything. They have lost their country, their culture, their language, a place to live and so many of their loved ones and children died in their escape to freedom.

Frank was helping me to remember that everyone has agreed to go through their Soul's journey and that was not my agreement in this lifetime. My agreement is to live the life I am living: to be the spiritual teacher and healer that I am, and that it is okay and very important to include myself in my prayers.

August 3, 2018

When I awoke this morning, the holy light was filling my body up with the golden white light. As it continued to fill me, I felt my heart open to a new sense of self-love. My whole body was filling up as my heart was releasing more and more self-love. I felt like I was home. I knew this love was who I was. I knew it through knowingness.

I had experienced this self-love many times, but this morning it was on a different level.

Last night as I was sitting in my living room, I felt a sense of love come over me, starting in my heart with a calm and peace and then moving through my whole body. I felt silent as I sat in the perfection of Oneness.

I had felt this many times over the last couple of years but don't remember feeling it since Frank's departure from this world.

This morning as I lay there in the divine essence of love, my man Jesus was with me and wanted me to walk with Him as I had done so many times in my life. He took me to the golden field where we met Frank.

They were showing me that the other day when I had fallen asleep and was gone for over four hours that I had been with them in the Spirit world. That is why when I awoke, I didn't know where I was and felt lighter.

Frank was explaining to me again that as he is shifting dimensions, that he is assisting me and many others to move into higher dimensions of themselves. As my vibration, my frequency, becomes higher, I will have a stronger connection with him in the higher dimensions and won't feel such a loss of him or separation of him on the Earth. We will merge together multidimensionally.

When I first started my spiritual work over thirty years ago, I channeled a spiritual Being named "White Lily." We taught classes and workshops together. I am not a trance channel, so I did not leave my body. She would be with me in my body. For many years she was my best friend and confidante. She constantly guided me.

Jesus had actually introduced her to me. After working together for some years, my teacher, Jesus, wanted me to integrate with her to be able to reach a larger audience.

At that time, I was teaching inner child healing through workshops at Unity Church, and I wanted to be able to teach inner child healing at more churches.

When Jesus asked me to integrate with White Lily, I felt a loss, while at the same time feeling myself more conscious and expanded within myself. I felt White Lily was activating higher aspects of me in other dimensions. Later, I understood that I was actually channeling myself; a higher aspect of myself that had integrated with me.

This is what Frank was explaining to me. He said that my spiritual work with others was going to expand into a higher consciousness because I was integrating with higher aspects of myself spiritually, in the Spirit world.

I know how important our thoughts are and how they affect us emotionally in this world and expand through all aspects of our bodies. Our thoughts affect our emotions, which shift our DNA systems. Much of my spiritual work is clearing and healing our emotions from all levels of our bodies mentally, emotionally and physically. As we release the old, hurtful emotions, our DNA actually shifts and activates our higher, God, Source DNA.

Jesus taught me how to open people's pineal glands and connect their gland to the heart of Mother, Father, Creator and into the Oneness from which we were first created.

From this place of Oneness, we then set the intention for whatever we want or need and then give thanks that it is done because in the higher dimensions it is. This energy is just raw,

Source energy and is going to support whatever our intentions may be.

Our pineal gland is in the center of our brain and is actually the Master cell, or connection, to the Source energy. As we set intentions, this Master cell communicates with all of the other cells in our bodies. It sends the frequency of our intentions to our cells. Our etheric body's DNA systems (energy body) then picks up the signal, or frequency, and matches and merges with the collective energy of this intention. This means that anyone else who has the same intention merges with our desires.

We actually match and merge with the morphogenetic and quantum field of our intentions. Our body lights up like a neon light and we draw back to ourselves like consciousness. Like attracts like.

I also know from my own healing experience and from working with others that when we have this much light downloaded and activated within us, this light will activate old, frozen emotions, or wounds, that need to be healed. The old emotions will surface to be healed.

We are multidimensional Beings, and the patterns we are clearing in this lifetime expand through all timelines of our Soul's journey. These patterns expand back into the Oneness before we became an individual Soul and seemingly separated from Source.

CHAPTER FOURTEEN

My Mother Heals our Relationship from the Spirit World

August 7, 2018

I had a dream about my mother and woke up with such a great understanding. In the dream she was showing me some papers. As I read them, I said to her that none of it made sense. All of the words were scrambled. She then left the room and I said to her husband, "I am not a licensed psychologist, so I don't know the correct terminology, but this is my work that I do with others."

There are a lot of energies here that are not light. This is old, karmic stuff. Then I stood up and walked into the next room. I looked out of a very big window, a sliding glass door and I saw my mother leaving. She was in a brown bathrobe and had a broom and dustpan. She was going to her other house. When I woke up and analyzed the dream, I understood that my mother was cleaning up everything karmic between us, my old hurts and wounds with her.

Since Frank's departure, my whole childhood with my mother has kept coming up. We had such a hard life together. I felt so unloved and invalidated by her. Up until she was on her death bed, she was still invalidating me. Her invalidation had really affected my self-worth. On her death bed, she validated me. As I was assisting her to leave this world, a couple of nights before she left, I asked her if she needed anything. She turned and looked into my eyes, Soul to Soul, and said to me, "Just you, sweetheart, and I really mean it." I felt it. I had waited my whole life for her to care about me and now, as she was leaving this world, she said goodbye to me in love.

Everything in the dream now made sense: the broom, the dustpan was cleaning us, cleaning the past, as she was going home into Spirit.

I realized why she has been with me, telling me it wasn't my time to go and why her energy stayed in me for a couple of weeks. She was holding me in my body so that I would not leave the Earth.

She was with me, loving me and supporting me to get through the loss of Frank.

As I am writing this, I feel her with me. I feel her love for me, and I can feel her smiling, like I get it. I am understanding emotionally our larger journey together.

After this experience, I once again was taken back to my childhood with my father, mother, and my paternal grandmother, Amy, who loved and adored me. I was the light of her life. My mother hated her and made no secret about it. Mom was always talking bad about her, and because of this I closed down my grandma's love for me. I felt guilty because she loved me so much and my mother hated her. I blocked my grandma's love for me to be able to survive the situation.

My mother would blame me and project her hatred and anger toward my grandmother on to me.

Not only had I compartmentalized the experience to survive it, I had also blocked myself from allowing love in.

My mother showed no love to me, and I felt guilty that my grandma loved me. I had created a belief that I wasn't worthy of love.

I am a very loving, caring woman. I usually see the higher picture of who a person or situation is and can very easily move out of judgements and into love for the person or circumstance.

In this moment, I was experiencing that although I had so much love for others, I had a hard time believing that I was worthy of love. Once again, my whole life was going before me, like a movie showing me all of the incidents in my life when I wouldn't really let love in and also how I had controlled and blocked myself from receiving love. I didn't think I was worthy of love. I had felt guilty if someone loved me. I remember so many times and incidents where people had honored me and told me that they loved me. I could see it but not feel it.

Now I knew why. I could feel the hurtful memories and frozen fear unraveling and releasing from my etheric DNA systems and bodies. I felt very peaceful and my sickness was subsiding. I could also see that so many of my past health problems had come from this agreement that I had made to myself. I wasn't worthy of love. I felt guilty if someone loved me. I could not receive it.

Frank and I were very close. I loved him very much. He was the man in my life on the Earth that I could really feel love with, and I knew he loved me. I held the light for him as he did for me. I always validated him from my heart.

My intention was to give my children what I didn't get. I wanted them to know regardless of what happened in life that I loved them.

My daughter said one of her last conversations with Frank was him telling her that he always felt loved by me. He always knew how much I loved him. He shared this in the hospital with her two nights before he left this world.

My workshops, teachings and books are always about self-love. Again, we teach what we need to heal. My favorite quote is 'Whatever the question, love is the answer.'

Because Frank and I were very close and we had the same spiritual understanding and consciousness, when he left, a big part of me, my heart, left with him. We were One heart, One soul.

This is why when he first left, I was also leaving with him, and why my mother came and told me it wasn't my time to go. She stayed with me to keep me in my body. Frank was the only man in my life that I was ever really connected to in the pure essence of love, unconditionally.

This is why when couples have been together for a long time, when one of them leaves, the other one leaves shortly afterwards; they become One heart. Like Carrie Fisher and Debbie Reynolds. When Carrie left, Debbie Reynolds willed herself to leave the next day. Debbie's son said he watched this happen.

I really did not realize until Frank left that he was the male energy, or man, in my life. He was also the man, male energy, for his sisters, Jennifer and Tricia and for his beloved daughter, Danilla.

As I am writing this, I can feel my mother's love and support with me now. I can feel her with Frank, and there is so much love and light between us all.

I also feel like I can get up and function again. I still feel like I have a cold, but I don't feel as sick, like I can't move. I actually feel the desire to go outside and take a little walk. I have the desire to participate in life again.

Frank was with me and telling me that I needed to get out of the house. He kept urging me.

I did force myself to get up and go to the store. I was very weak and emotional.

When I got to my favorite grocery store, the very first person I saw was a woman named Mary. I knew now why Frank was urging me, hurrying me up; it was because he wanted me to run into Mary. He had planned it for me, for us.

Mary

Mary is a woman who contacted me shortly after Frank left. She had also lost her son. He made his transition back into the Spirit world three years before Frank.

An acquaintance of mine had invited me to her husband's celebration of life. He had just passed away. I responded with my own circumstances of Frank leaving. Because it was a group email, many received my reply and Mary immediately reached out to me. She wanted to assist me through my grief and loss in any way that she could.

I was very grateful for her love and support, but when I returned to Sedona I had not reached out to her.

Frank was at it again, assisting from the other side. He wanted me to run into Mary in the grocery store. This is why Frank was very insistent that I get out of the house for a while. He knew that I would meet Mary.

Mary invited me for breakfast at her home. Frank and Mary's son immediately showed up and were both very present during our time together. It was pretty amazing to have both of our sons communicating with us from the spirit world. Mary also had a direct communication with her son as I did with Frank. We laughed a lot with our boys during our time together.

Because Mary had been down the road of loss that I was embarking on, she was able to help me and also gave me permission to go through and understand the many layers of grief and loss.

Because of my spiritual understanding, it seemed people expected me to be in the higher consciousness of Frank's departure. Although I had an understanding and belief that it was Frank's time to go, as a mother on the Earth plane, losing my son was heartbreaking.

Mary understood this because she also had a higher connection to the Spirit world and yet losing her son, her only child, was at the time, unbearable.

Mary was such a great gift in my life, and I am forever grateful that she reached out to me and that Frank guided me to run into her at the grocery store.

August 12, 2018

When I awoke this morning, once again the holy light was filling the room and penetrating me.

My heart was so full of love and was filling and expanding my whole body with love. All I could feel was love and gratitude, not for any reason, just for being. With every breath I took I could feel more waves of love filling me and expanding me into the One collective love energy or frequency.

As I continued to expand into and through love's frequency, my thoughts went to my mother. I could once again feel her with me and all I could feel towards her and for her was love and gratitude.

I felt so much joy and freedom and said out loud, "My mother is my hero!"

From the other side or from the higher dimensions, beyond our earthly agreements, she was absolutely there for me, loving, supporting and validating me.

Although I knew her life on the Earth had not been easy, I now had the opportunity to experience who she really was and how much she loved me.

My mother had stepped up to the higher calling from the Spirit world and was healing our life together. She had kept me in my body, to help me heal and release our life together, so I could go forward into the next step of my Soul's journey on

Earth. She was freeing me into my new lifetime on the Earth without physically leaving the body.

As I mentioned before, my dad who had PTSD from WWII, would flip out, feel remorse and leave. My mother had total responsibility for us.

There were five of us kids, and of course, our collie dog. My mother worked two jobs to support us. She was always exhausted and upset. As a child, I didn't understand this, and as a teenager I was actually glad that she wasn't home much. When she was home, she was so tired. This gave me the opportunity to go out and stay out late because she would never wake up when I came home. She never knew what time I got home. Because of my mother, we always lived in a nice place, had food to eat, and dressed fairly nicely.

In the days that she was raising us, welfare and food stamps were not available. She did it on her on.

All five of us kids have turned out to be very hard workers. We are survivors and really good, caring, loving people.

CHAPTER FIFTEEN

My New Past Life with Frank

August 15, 2018

I woke up this morning with Frank speaking to me from the Spirit world. He was explaining to me that the life we had shared together on Earth was becoming a past life ... and we are moving into a new lifetime together. I am in Spirit guiding you and you agreed to stay on the Earth to guide many into higher understandings and dimensions of themselves. Only now your audience is in a bigger agreement as is mine.

My departure was not an accident. I moved back into Spirit to expand into myself multidimensionally so I could also reach a larger audience in my healing work. When I shifted dimensions, I assisted many to shift with me, into a higher understanding of their own inner light, magnificence, what is important in life, and into their higher purpose on the Earth.

Mom, imagine taking us into a past life like you do when you are working with others. See and experience us and our whole family unit standing on a stage together bowing to an audience that is giving us a standing ovation. Cut the karmic cords between us, everyone on the stage, everyone in the audience, and do Soul retrieval. Send everyone's energy back to them and bring your energy connected to everyone else back into you.

See this as a play, as a movie, and what a great job we all did together. We all completed in love and gratitude, with, and for each other. That was our Soul's purpose. We completed in love.

You agreed to stay on the Earth for me to be able to work

through you and with you, to assist many in their Soul's Awakening, in their higher purpose on Earth.

You are on a plateau clearing out more of your old, emotional, karmic energy to make room for more of your higher understanding and the collective awakening.

I love you, mom. Thank you for agreeing to be my mother, for opening the door for me to move into myself, my own self-love, and to experience and see all on the Earth as love. Whoever they are or whatever they have done, they—we, are all children or aspects of the One Source of love, of God-Creation.

I am now giving my love and support back to you. We are one Soul and have agreed to work together. Everything we have gone through in this lifetime has prepared us for what lies ahead in the larger picture of all consciousness.

I love you, Mama. Frank.

August 19, 2018

I awoke this Sunday morning with what I call the holy light filling my room and body.

I could feel beautiful music. I couldn't hear it but could feel my body responding to the frequency of the sound-music.

Frank was here and wanted me to walk with him in the higher dimensions of prayer. I walked with him into multidimensional colors where I could see huge columns of light. The columns were very solid light structures that had a huge base but did not connect to a ceiling.

As I walked through this dimension with Frank, he was showing me this was one of many prayer temples. What I had been feeling was the beautiful sound of prayer. These prayer temples are situated throughout the higher dimensions, much like us on the Earth having many different churches, synagogues, mosques and temples all over the world.

The difference being, in the higher Spiritual realms, there is only one celebration of God / Source / I AM / Oneness / All is One; there are not different religions, or beliefs, like we have on the Earth.

Souls in the Spirit world also go to these different temples to give prayer and to receive prayer. When we pray for our loved ones in Spirit, their Souls receive the prayer as a positive energy, and it actually assists to rethread their Soul's energy into a higher completion with whomever is praying for them. Prayer is energy, and because there is no time or distance, prayer feeds the Soul.

While on the Earth, Frank practiced Ho'oponopono, an old Hawaiian prayer. In this prayer we understand that we are One consciousness, not separate from each other. In the Spirit world, we receive prayer in this way. When we pray for a Soul that is no longer on the Earth, our love and the person's love come together in a mutual healing. This one love starts healing and clearing up old, karmic, emotional agreements and contracts.

It is never too late to heal with someone. Even if they are in the Spirit world, as we pray from the core of our heart's love and ask for forgiveness or give forgiveness, a great healing takes place for both or all of us. The person (or persons) receives it, and the receiving of this love then ripples back to us on Earth. A freedom and freeing of the old takes place, so that we on the Earth can move forward.

Souls on the other side also pray for us. They see and experience what we go through down here on Earth, like my mother seeing that I was getting ready to leave and stepped in and stopped it from happening.

It is never too late to heal relationships. Our loved ones are still very much with us. They have just changed addresses or shifted dimensions. They are not in a physical body, but they are a Soul that keeps growing emotionally as we do on Earth. They experience life from a higher lens of perception, but their hearts are very much connected to ours.

August 20, 2018
Broken pieces

Frank has been connecting with me, but I feel too tired to respond. I have so little energy. My house is a mess and I can't muster up the energy to clean it. I just pray that no one comes over without calling.

I lay on the sofa in my living room, and I feel like I am broken. As I said, I never really comprehended what that felt or meant until now. Like many of you who have agreed to wake up spiritually, my journey in life has not been easy, but with the help of God, Spirit, Jesus, I have always been able to pick myself up and get through it.

Now, I still have my spiritual team with me, but I can't pick myself up, put myself back together to function. I definitely feel broken and shattered in pieces, so fragmented that I feel as though I am blown apart.

I always felt as though I had an energetic pattern in life or a journey, a destiny. I didn't always know what it was, but with Spirit I could always pick myself up and go forward.

I now feel like that pattern, life's programs or agreements, have been blasted open, and I have lost my groove or wherever I am supposed to connect to go forward.

I feel like Humpty Dumpty that fell off the wall and am shattered into a million pieces.

Because of my spiritual work, in my mind I know this is temporary, but emotionally, I am shattered.

Grief is a very debilitating process. I don't know when the emotional waves will surface or when they will break so I can go forward again.

Frank is with me, telling me that I am in the middle of an emotional wave, like the ocean's waves. When in the middle of a wave, there is not much a person can do but ride it until it breaks. As the wave breaks, it either pulls you under or pushes you forward.

I knew in my mind how much Frank loved the ocean. He was a surfer boy. I used to joke and say his greatest goal in life was to catch the biggest wave.

Most of the pictures I have of Frank are in front of or in the ocean, in some way.

Now in my heart, I experience his love of the ocean. He always said surfing for him was his meditation; he was with God. I can feel it, and I see and feel him in Spirit in all of the beautiful dimensions. They flow together like the ocean waves, only much softer. They look like clouds and the colors blend and merge into each other. I think when he was surfing, he was actually riding the dimensional waves in Spirit. He was on the Earth and remembering his life in the Spirit world.

CHAPTER SIXTEEN

Breaking Through a "Dark Night of the Soul"

August 21, 2018

Today I woke up to thunder and storms. I felt so much peace and gratitude. Something had shifted since yesterday. I still lacked energy, but I was peaceful.

I decided to lay there and see if I could communicate with Frank. I could feel him around me, but he was not communicating. I thought he must be busy elsewhere.

I did not want to lose the beautiful feeling of peace and decided to give myself a healing session.

I followed the energy back to when I was 33 years old. At the time, I thought I was having a breakdown, but it was actually a breakthrough.

I was sick and couldn't work. I had been sick for a few months before the doctor could find out what was wrong. I had surgery and went on disability. My boyfriend, who I had been living with, and I split up. I could no longer afford to live where I was, and my mother suggested that I put everything in storage and come live with her. I had an eight-year-old daughter who I needed to get in school. My mother lived in Sacramento, California. Our living together lasted two days.

From there, I ended up living with my brother and his wife in Santa Cruz, California. I was sick, could not take care of myself, and I didn't really have a place to live. I was so emotionally torn up over my relationship with my mother.

I wrote my mother a letter and said that anyone in my life, who I can allow to affect me the way I allow you, I can no longer have in my life; I divorced her.

This was the first time in my life that I couldn't take care of myself. I had been on my own since I was 16 years old.

Before I moved in with my two-day stay with my mother, my then 16-year-old daughter ran away with her boyfriend. I was heartbroken; history was repeating itself. I had worked so hard to break the patterns.

At the same time, all of this was happening, my Aunt Cecil, who had been my rock, died, and a friend of mine who I had known in Oregon was murdered.

My whole life or foundation came crashing down and at the time I wasn't emotionally strong enough to put myself back together.

When I moved to Santa Cruz, Frank, who had been living with his father for a couple of years, wanted to move back in with me. My brother, my hero, rented me a house so that could happen. By this time, my disability had run out, and I had to go on welfare. To be eligible for welfare, I had to register at the unemployment office and look for a job.

As I look back now, this all seems humorous, definitely another lifetime. I still remember my counselor at the unemployment office. As she was interviewing me, she stopped, looked at me, and very caringly said, "I really think you need some more time."

I also started seeing a therapist who suggested that I needed additional help and sent me to a women's support group.

This helped me tremendously. She extended her hand and started pulling me out of my "Dark Night of the Soul." I was talking to someone who had somewhat of an understanding of what was happening to me. I didn't have a clue. I was very depressed. I remember laying on the bed crying and Frank sat on the bed with me. He was telling me what a great mother I was and had always been, that I was always looking for ways for us to heal and to have a better life.

Like most people, I wanted my children to have a better life than I had lived.

At 26, I had moved to Hawaii from California with three children. Frank came home in Hawaii. He had a Hawaiian heart and Soul.

I had been a brownie leader, and in Hawaii became a cub scout leader and room mother and was very involved in my children's lives. I got a big brother for Frank when we moved to Hawaii. (Making the move to Hawaii was the best move I had ever made. I was going to the University of Hawaii and after four years in Hawaii, I decided to move to Eugene, Oregon where I was born. I wanted to attend the University of Oregon. They had a very good psychology department.

At that time, my two older children moved to Santa Cruz, California to live with their father. When I moved to Santa Cruz with my brother, Frank was already there and immediately moved back in with me.)

I felt safe in this women's support group. This was a very supportive group, and the therapist suggested and assisted me to get into the battered women's shelter, to get away from the man who I had broken up with, and to have support from women.

Frank was 14 at the time. He and his friends loaded up my rental truck with my belongings, and they helped me put everything into storage.

One of Frank's friend's mother called me and said that they, her family, wanted to take Frank until I could get my life back on track.

I was so grateful and let her know that I would pay her back when I was able. She said she didn't want me to pay her back. That when they were younger and having a difficult time, someone had helped them and when I was able, they wanted me to pay it forward and help someone else.

As I look back at that breakthrough in my life, (At the time I thought it was a breakdown.) it was one of the greatest gifts of my life.

I have so much compassion for people who are homeless and are going through challenging times. Never in my life did I think I would end up with no place to live, to not be able to work, and certainly not living in a battered woman's shelter.

Jobs had always come easily for me, and I had always been able to afford to live in nice homes. This very humbling breakthrough changed and shifted my life in ways I could not imagine.

While living in the women's shelter, a few of the women were enrolled in a holistic college in Santa Cruz called Heartwood.

Jesus told me to enroll in the college. I somewhat protested. I didn't even know what holistic health meant. I did not have any money and no place to live. Jesus said to enroll! I always follow orders from what I call headquarters and enrolled.

I told my brother that I had enrolled in a holistic health college, and unknown to me, he shared the information with my mother.

I was very surprised to hear my mother's voice on the phone. She called and offered to pay my way. I was shocked and surprised. This was her way of starting to heal our relationship.

As a child I can't remember anyone telling me that I was loved or anyone even touching me.

At Heartwood, I started doing massage, and all the layers of frozen fear, emotions, started erupting like a volcano letting go of lifetimes of hurt. When I started massaging people, I was able to scan their bodies, and I could see inside their second chakra and their whole childhood started running by me like a movie. I was shown what it was like in their mother's womb, where they started picking up their belief systems and patterns.

I was shown their beginning patterns with their mother and father and what it was like before they came down into this lifetime. As I looked at the hurtful emotions stored in their bodies, I was shown how these unhealed emotions affected the health of their whole body, mentally, emotionally and physically. From there, I started taking people into past lives that were holding the patterns and programs intact in this lifetime.

When we went into the lifetime to heal and clear the patterns, we would also do Soul retrieval and bring aspects of their Soul that had been left behind into them now. People started having miraculous healings, as was I.

I was then shown how to release entities (other Souls connected to people) back into the light or highest from where they came.

From there, I started doing inner child healing and workshops taking people back into their mother's womb. I connected them with their little girl or boy to see and experience exactly where their patterns began controlling their lives.

Again, we did Soul retrieval, and they learned how to love and reparent their inner children.

As my spiritual healing journey continued to awaken, my whole spiritual team started aligning with me, Archangel Michael was one of the first to step forward to show me how to protect myself and how to cut emotional cords. He and Jesus work very much together. I still have the same team today; only they have expanded their circle allowing many more high, spiritual Beings to assist.

Spirituality has always been my life, my purpose and passion. Frank was right; I was always looking for ways to heal myself and my children.

Out of nowhere one day when Frank was about eight, he said to me, "Gosh mom, can you see as you are healing that even Grandma and Grandpa are healing?" I believe we teach what we need to heal, and from my own healing I experienced my whole family unit starting to heal.

And now, Jesus had led me to the holistic health college to heal, clear and release many of my own patterns and programs. He knew that I needed to be able to see and understand people's bodies so that I could move on to the next step of my Soul's purpose on the Earth, which is a healer.

At the time, I also started teaching small, spiritual groups.

While in the woman's shelter, one of the counselors told me of a house to rent that was very close to her, which I rented and moved into.

Four years after my breakthrough, I moved back to Hawaii and very quickly became one of the top spiritual healers on Oahu. My life has continued to expand and open up to many different healing modalities.

Jesus is still my main man and confidante, and I am very grateful to have his continued love and support.

August 23, 2018
Experiencing a Support Group

Being back in Sedona has been very hard for me. I don't have the love and support system that I have in Sweden. It is hard because Frank used to call me all the time just to let me know that he loved me and to share with me his amazing spiritual journey. He would call me to share about all of the amazing people he was meeting and helping just by loving them, accepting them totally for who they were and of course his forgiveness. He absolutely saw each person he met as an aspect of himself and the purity of God, and the more he could love and accept them, the more he could love and accept himself.

I have had a few friends reach out to me that I am very grateful for. One friend would text me almost daily and ask me how I was doing that day.

Just this small act of love and kindness was very important to me. I felt like I had a lifeline to hold onto. I felt like someone cared and I wasn't so alone.

People really don't know what to say or do when you lose someone you love, especially a child. Because of this, many times, they avoid you.

It meant so much to me just to have someone checking in. There really isn't anything anyone can do to take the pain away. It is a journey each person must go through.

I decided to go to a grief support group here in Sedona. As soon as I walked into the room, I wanted to leave but did not want to be disrespectful. I felt much worse when I finally did leave.

There were only about five of us in the group. These people had been meeting for about 20 years. The woman to my right came in eating doughnuts and she weighed about three hundred pounds. She kept complaining about how much her legs hurt. She was very heavy and was using a cane because she was having a hard time walking.

We went around the circle and each person shared their story, and every time someone shared, she would butt in and tell more of her story.

The other people in the group had lost their loved ones about 20 years ago. I could hardly breathe with all this stuck energy. I felt like they were supporting each other to stay stuck in their grief.

Every time the woman to my right would butt in, people just allowed her to take over the group. No one said anything to her.

I started having a sense of unreality. Is this really happening? Is this really a support group? Suddenly, I felt like I could not comprehend what I was experiencing. I felt like I was in the movie 'One Flew Over the Cuckoo's Nest.'

I am a spiritual healer and counselor. One of my specialties is to assist people to move through their painful, frozen, hurtful emotions - to move through the experience and into the light at the end - or at least to be able to function much easier.

Here I was in Sedona, AZ, one of the highest spiritual meccas of the world where you have every kind of healer, therapist, hypnotherapist, etc. that you could imagine, and I am in a support group that is totally unconscious.

Suddenly, my mother from the Spirit world breaks my spell and says to me, "Boy, we sure know what she does to numb her feelings and emotions. She eats." That was definitely my mother's humor. It would have been funny had it not been so tragic. She was talking about the woman to my right who had not stopped eating or talking since the support group began.

When I left the group, I felt worse than when I had gone in, but my mother's spirit stayed with me, which helped.

I have talked to people that have gone to amazing grief support groups, but this was not one of them. For those of you who are in grief, I strongly suggest that you reach out to support groups. We definitely need each other to get through this kind of loss. Even with my spiritual understanding, this has been the hardest lesson of my life.

CHAPTER SEVENTEEN

Forgiving Frank for Leaving

September 8, 2018

I asked Frank to come to me in a dream He had not appeared to me in a dream, and I was surprised that he hadn't.

Last night it happened. I can't remember the first part, but we were in a car, and Frank was driving. We stopped in front of the beach, the one that he loved to surf in Hawaii.

I said, "This isn't where we're supposed to meet the person." Whoever that was.

Frank stood in front of the wall looking down on the ocean and said how much he loved the Earth and how beautiful it is here.

He was dressed in white, the way he has shown himself to me in the Spirit world.

He was breathing in the ocean air and wanted me to breathe it in also. The wind was blowing, and Frank was so beautiful, handsome and vibrant. He looked just the way he looked before he got sick. He was very real, very much alive. He took his shirt off to feel and breathe in the wind and warmth of the sun on his skin.

He was telling me what a good life I had ahead of me, here on Earth.

He said he could only stay for a few minutes that someone was coming to pick him up soon

He was sharing again how much he loved the Earth: how the Earth's beauty was so breathtaking; the green mountains and I could feel the green. We were standing near Diamond Head

Volcano in Honolulu, and the mountain was very green. It had been raining a lot.

Then I woke up and was still very much in the dream, while I was awake. He said it is very different in the Spirit world, also beautiful but different. Spirit is love unconditional. Love is not something that one had to think about; it just is - our true state of being. The Spirit world is more etheric, very colorful but a very different energy. It's not the contrast that one experiences on the Earth.

He explained what a privilege it is to be on the Earth and how much a Soul gets to experience here. He had loved the Earth, the ocean, nature, and all the beauty. The Earth is sharper, more contrast, a different sense of life force. He loved it and was grateful to be able to experience it again for these few minutes with me.

He looked at me with so much love. He was love, like he was on the Earth, but his earthly lessons were over, and in some way the love was more intact. He is a whole Being, body and Soul vibrating in a very strong Knowing of love. I felt my whole body fill with love, and we became One Soul of Knowing, not knowing what I knew but knowing that I knew what he was sharing with me without words.

He then said that I knew it was his time to leave and I really needed to remember that, to focus on the larger picture of our purpose together.

I have been having health challenges. I have IBS. It hasn't bothered me much over the last few years, because I am conscious of what I eat, and I know how to deal with it, what to take to help it.

The last few days my intestines have been so painful, sometimes unbearable. I have been doubling over in pain and cannot stand up straight. My intestinal pain is pulling my whole body forward.

I was also aware that the condition was becoming serious and was wondering if I should go to the emergency room at the hospital.

In 2004 while in India, I actually went through a near death experience from the same problem. I know that the intestines (our gut) also have a brain and are affected by our emotions. I am also aware that the loss of Frank, and all of my emotions surrounding his leaving, have affected my intestines.

I have been sending love and light to my intestines, and nothing is shifting.

Frank looked at me and said, "Mom, your intestinal pain is because you have not forgiven me for leaving. Mom, you need to forgive me for leaving." I stood frozen; my body was frozen. I didn't realize I blamed him for leaving. I do remember feeling anger at him for leaving, but I just thought it was part of my grief process.

As he stood before me, I knew he had come to help me through the healing process, and I could not say the words: "I forgive you for leaving." The higher part, and my intellectual part of me, knew that it was his time, but the human mother me was stuck emotionally in unforgiveness. I had no idea of this.

Frank's whole life was about love and forgiveness. He had come to me because he knew I was stuck emotionally in not being able to forgive him, but the human me didn't even know I was stuck there.

I haven't been able to write or work on the book in a few weeks, and I didn't know why until now. I was savoring this time with him, and I loved hearing his voice as he talked to me.

I love his laughter, his sense of freedom, as he stood there in the wind listening to the ocean waves crashing. He was also breathing in the experience. He also wanted me to tell Danilla that he is always with her, that he is her guardian angel, and that he loves her very much. He is very proud of the beautiful, young woman that she is becoming.

He then told me that he had to leave. Frank was laughing and stuck out his thumb like he was hitchhiking, and he was gone.

I also know what my assignment is today: to give myself a healing session and go into forgiveness. As I write this I am saying, "Frank, I forgive you for leaving me. For leaving us." And I started sobbing. When I stood up, I felt better. My intestines felt better.

I know from the spiritual work that I do with others that frozen emotions affect the physical body. Many times, the experience or pain is so great that we compartmentalize the experience to move through it. The frozen emotions, stories, hidden memories affect our physical bodies.

None of us really realized that Frank was the man, or male energy, in our lives, the glue that somehow held us together, until he was no longer here. My two daughters, my sister who was very close with Frank, his ex-wife, his daughter Danilla, and myself — all female - and Frank was the glue in some way that bound us all together with his male, loving, caring, protective energy.

Frank loved all of us and always called us to let us know how much he loved us. He was so enthusiastic about life and always had beautiful suggestions of love to assist us in our day to day lives. He was not controlling but would stop anyone who was starting to go into negativity.

He was Mr. Positive and always saw the best in life, in everybody, and in most situations.

September 10, 2018
Experiencing a Healing From Forgiving Frank

Yesterday after voicing the words of forgiving Frank for leaving, my intestines instantly started feeling better. They were still tender but nothing like the pain I had experienced for a few days.

Today my intestines were doing better, but I was still having a hard time standing up straight. When I looked in the mirror, I saw a bent over, old lady. My God, I thought. What happened to me? I was still having a hard time standing and was too weak to exercise. I had lost so much weight, and my skin was hanging in places; I hardly recognized myself.

I could feel Frank with me and knew that I needed to give myself a healing session to release from me my unforgiveness of Frank leaving. I started the session forgiving Frank for leaving, and all of the other emotions that I had experienced during the eight years since Frank had been diagnosed with being sick started surfacing. I started feeling all of my pent-up emotion of anger that I had felt because I had thought he needed to be more proactive in his healing process. As I was cleaning out his apartment, I actually saw paperwork showing that he was very active in his attempt to get on the transplant list.

My anger and confusion was my belief that he hadn't done more to get on the transplant list. He needed to do so much to make that happen, and I wanted him to do it faster.

I didn't realize that I blamed him for his death. I started forgiving every emotional experience that I had gone through. I just kept saying, "Frank, I forgive you" for everything that kept coming up. As I was going through the process, I could feel the stuck energy, the emotions releasing from all levels of my body.

As I was continuing the process, my whole life with Frank started surfacing again.

My subconscious mind was Googling up other stories, experiences and emotions that we needed to heal.

As our history continued to reveal itself, I kept forgiving him and then all of the guilt of my lifetime with him started surfacing. I then started asking him to forgive me and I started forgiving myself. I continued to feel the old emotions releasing from my body. They were actually like thread unravelling from my bodies and systems.

As I was nearing the end of my forgiveness journey with Frank, I started seeing pictures of experiences with my mother from this lifetime.

I could feel and see my mother with Frank from the other side. I went through the same healing, forgiveness journey with my mother. Once again, my subconscious mind was googling up our old stories for me to forgive, heal and release.

I could also feel the energies of my forgiveness process with my mother releasing from my bodies.

Frank told me to tear up all of the pictures of him being sick. I had matched and merged with the emotions of him being sick, how much he had aged and it was pulling my systems into aging also. Once again, Frank told me to tear up all pictures that I had of him being sick. Every time I looked at the pictures, I would cry and think what happened to my beautiful boy? His body had deteriorated so quickly.

When I was done with the healing process, I gently stood up and found myself standing very erect and tall.

Through forgiveness I had cleared the sick, death emotions out of my bodies and systems and I felt light and free.

In my spiritual understanding, I believe we choose our lifetimes and the lessons we agree to go through, to learn and heal with each other.

In the higher picture, there is nothing to forgive, but in our life together on the Earth, we have many emotions that we need to forgive, heal, and clear not just from this lifetime but from many lifetimes together. All of the emotions from all lifetimes are in our physical bodies now.

The Creator says this is the lifetime that we have agreed to come full circle. Every lesson, person, and experience we go through has a frame of reference someplace else, meaning past life or even earlier in this lifetime. It could be patterns that you picked up while in your mother's womb, and you are now playing them out to heal and release for yourself and your ancestors. You might be the light one, many times feeling like the black sheep child in your family unit, who has agreed to heal and clear ancestor patterns. As you release the patterns from yourself, a domino effect happens and you start unraveling or releasing them for your entire family unit.

My suggestion is for you to lie down and start forgiving anyone with whom you are out of balance; all memories will come up for you to forgive, heal and release. This will start freeing you from sickness, disease, and will shift you into your higher purpose, and the higher frequencies of this lifetime on Earth. Because like attracts like you will bring higher consciousness into your new life on all levels.

Forgive. Forgive. And Forgive some more. Make sure you forgive yourself for not knowing better. This level of forgiveness shifts you out of victim consciousness and into gratitude for everyone and everything.

September 11, 2018

The last week has been such an incredible shift in consciousness or realities.

Going through the forgiveness with Frank and my mother absolutely cleared my body. I have always taught that our frozen or unhealed emotions affect our physical body creating sickness, disease. While I was going through the release, I could feel the old, painful emotions unraveling from my body and systems like a ball of string opening up. I could feel the fear emotions start to unravel from my legs, from my calves, moving up clearing my thighs, and as the emotions started clearing from my intestines, I could feel the light, and a warmth of love fill the spaces that had emptied.

I could breathe easier; my breath could actually move into my intestines, and I felt peace fill the areas that had been so locked in fear.

Yesterday, I felt like I needed to go to my doctor because I felt like I had a low-grade infection. I have had diverticulitis for years but have never had a bout with it as seriously as this one has been.

Although I was feeling much better, I was concerned that leakage from my intestines could have gone into my system, and I wanted to have bloodwork done to make sure I was okay.

When my doctor examined me, she touched the area and it was too sensitive for me to allow her to put any pressure on it.

She was very concerned because she could feel a little bulge and because of my pain, she said that I should go to emergency right away, that my intestine could burst. I knew this but was feeling so much better than I had been feeling.

She insisted I go to emergency and have tests done to make sure I was going to be okay. She called emergency and told them I was on my way. When I got to the emergency clinic, they were really full and busy, and I got the last room available.

After me, two more people came into the emergency room and were put on beds in the hallway. After the nurse hooked me up to an IV and drew blood, the doctor came in to explain that he was having x-rays done of my intestines and that a dye would be injected into me through the IV, but he wanted to make sure my kidneys and organs were healthy enough for the dye to go through my body (which they were). He said it would be a while before I went in for x-rays.

The emergency room was very noisy with so much activity.

As I lay there, my man Jesus came to me and informed me

that he was going to heal me. He took me back to a memory of Frank as a child.

After Frank's third kidney surgery, his doctor told me that he was sure Frank was going to lose his left kidney, but he wanted to wait six weeks to see if there was any improvement.

At that time, Jesus came to me and told me he was going to heal Frank's kidneys. With him, through intention, we sent healing energy to Frank's kidneys.

As I explained before, when we went back to his doctor six weeks later (after new x-rays were taken), his doctor told me that it was a miracle, that the kidney had healed itself. He had other doctors look at the x-rays, and they all had a hard time believing it had healed.

This is also when I started my healing journey with Jesus. As I lay in the hospital bed in the emergency room, Jesus was telling me that now he was going to heal me.

I walked with him into an etheric dimension that was very clear, just pure energy, or consciousness. There was no thought, just pure Source energy. Through intention he sent energy into my whole system and all of the emotional stories of my life started surfacing, shifting out of emotions and out of my bodies, like clouds clearing and disappearing.

As this was happening, I felt very peaceful as I drifted into total love for all, for everything. I could feel silent music fill me up, meaning I couldn't hear the sound, the frequency, but could certainly feel this beautiful music fill up the spaces where the old, emotional stories had lived in my body.

My body, mentally, emotionally and physically seemed to be vibrating as One body in peace and harmony. I was floating in love.

Although the noise in the emergency room was going on around me, I could not hear any of it. I could only feel love, peace and harmony.

As I started floating back from this dimension and into the hospital room, I put my hand on the bulge and the pain on my side had totally disappeared as well as the bulge. There was no bulge or pain.

At that time, the nurse came back into the room and apologized for all of the noise and confusion. I had not heard any of it.

Another nurse came in and wheeled me into the x-ray room. I knew nothing would be found, but I also wanted proof for myself. I was also feeling, wondering, did that really happen? The healing?

While back in my room awaiting the x-ray result, my man Jesus came to me again and asked me to walk with him. We went to a beautiful, green, flower-filled garden. I could feel how alive it was, and I could smell the flowers and life force. As we neared the center of the garden, I could see my whole family waiting for us, everyone that was on the other side in Spirit.

Of course, I could see Frank and my mom first. They were my welcoming committee. As I walked farther into the center, I could see both of my grandmothers, my aunt, my dad, my cousins and other relatives.

They welcomed me and I could feel love, laughter, and so much joy and completion between all of us. I also experienced the different roles that we had agreed to play with each other while on the Earth together. I was experiencing most of this through knowingness. We were communicating through thought, not the spoken word.

Then Jesus started talking to me and shared that I was complete with my whole family, complete karmically and that I was now moving into a new lifetime on the Earth without physically leaving the body. Basically, everyone here with me now would be a past life for me.

This is the information the Creator had been talking about, sharing through me for many years, that we are coming into a new lifetime without physically leaving the body. We are shifting dimensions. We are clearing out the old, hurtful patterns, contracts, and agreements and are moving into higher aspects of ourselves multidimensionally.

Of course, many people like Frank are also leaving the planet.

As I stood there with everyone, I actually felt a loss, a completion, or death of all of it. I especially didn't want to leave my mother. Now that she is on the other side, we have become best friends. My mother has been with me ever since Frank's departure from this world. She actually stepped in and has kept me here, in my body on the Earth.

My mother then promised me that she would be with me, stay with me as I continued to transition into my new lifetime on Earth. And of course Frank would be with me continuing to guide me and work with me in my workshops and sessions.

I could feel so much love, support and gratitude from everyone and then well wishes and blessings as I continued my newer, higher, Soul's Awakening on the Earth.

What an amazing experience. I was in many dimensions at once, deaths of old patterns, completions and the rebirth of a whole new journey. I had no idea where it was going to lead me, but I did know it was going to be wonderful and magical.

I was so full of love and gratitude that when the doctor came in to tell me that everything was fine, that nothing could be found that was creating the pain and discomfort, all I could do was smile ear to ear.

I could not really talk, just shook my head in understanding and gratefulness. As I looked at him, I could see what a beautiful light Soul he was and that he was definitely fulfilling his Soul's purpose of service. He was a very kind, caring doctor, man. And of course, all of my tests including bloodwork were fine, perfect.

When I got in to my car to drive home, I felt stunned, not in a bad way but so expanded within myself that I felt like I didn't quite belong here on Earth and yet, I was here to share my story to assist others and to move forward in my new lifetime's journey.

When I looked around me, all I could see was beauty: beauty in the sky, clouds, and the red rocks. Everything was very much alive. Now I understood why Frank loved the Earth so much, its beauty.

I was seeing and experiencing my surroundings through a higher lens of perception, the perception that my beautiful son had always experienced. It took me a little while to ground myself with my new lifetime's frequency before I could drive home.

Today, as I look back at yesterday, I still feel the higher frequencies and also know that I could not have shifted out of my pain had I not gone into the level of forgiveness that Frank had taken me into.

I really had no idea that those kinds of hurtful emotions were still in me, or what the Creator calls frozen emotions. These old, frozen, fear emotions are actually the glue that holds our old patterns in place. Until we forgive, we can't move onto the highest of what our Soul has agreed to do or accomplish in this lifetime.

The emotions are energy patterns that we took on to heal and clear in this lifetime. As we go into and release the frozen emotions, we release the patterns and our life becomes easier, lighter and more joyful.

Sometimes we have to go through a "Dark Night of the Soul" to get there, but we are the light at the end of the tunnel.

Thank you, God — Spirit - my whole spiritual team - my ancestors in Spirit and on the Earth. Thank you, mom, and thank you my beautiful son, Frank. Thank you, Frank, for agreeing to leave this world to open the door for me and for so many to move into the higher perspective and purpose of our lives.

I love you forever and ever, my beautiful boy. Thank you for choosing me as your mother this time around. It has truly been an honor and a privilege.

September 20, 2018
It's Final — Frank is Gone

The last couple of days have been very hard and emotional. So much grief and loss is surfacing again.

My daughter, sister and Frank's ex-wife are finishing up, clearing everything out of Frank's apartment so it can be rented out. Jennifer loaded his truck with all of his tools and had it shipped to the Big Island (Hawaii) where she lives. This is such a completion of his earthly life. It is final — complete — he is really gone.

September 21, 2018
Frank Assisting Souls Reincarnating to the Earth

When I woke up this morning, Mother Mary came and wanted me to walk with her. We walked through beautiful gardens that were so alive that the flowers were actually singing together, I could feel their harmony and love. We then walked up a hill to a huge, outdoor pavilion filled with many people. It seemed like we were at some kind of seminar, and the people seemed very excited and enthusiastic about what was being taught. As I looked to my right, in front of all of those people, I could see Frank. Mother Mary wanted me to see Frank in his new role. He may have left his earthly body role, but he was very much alive. Frank was the teacher, educating these Souls about how different the Earth is compared to the Spiritual realms.

These were Souls that were getting ready to reincarnate to the Earth. Some of them had not been on the Earth in quite a while.

Many of these Souls are very high spiritual Beings of light.

Some are Spirit guides and teachers that are agreeing to lower their vibration to come down to the Earth.

They are the Souls (children) being born fully conscious of God, Spirit and a higher understanding of life. As children, they are amazing teachers of light that are assisting everyone around them to wake up and heal. They are actually portals of light that affect everyone that they come in contact with.

They are born with all veils lifted between themselves and the Spirit worlds and are living from their higher selves. Because of them I feel like our world will be in good hands. They are the future of our world. These high conscious Souls are coming to the Earth as guiding lights, teachers, to assist humanity out of our collective "Dark Night of the Soul" and back into what is important in life: love and compassion.

Frank was explaining to everyone what the Earth and its inhabitants are going through right now. He was explaining that he had just come back from the Earth, that he had come down to go through a refresher course to once again feel and understand the emotions that earthlings go through.

I felt so happy to see him again and very proud to experience the high level of work that he is doing in the other dimensions. He is a very powerful teacher and guide for many.

CHAPTER EIGHTEEN

Sweden – Short Tour /
The Non-Believer Believes

November 13, 2018

I was speaking tonight and facilitating a group healing from Spirit for all participants. Once again, I could feel everyone's love and support for me. I felt very raw and when I mentioned Frank I cried. I have worked with and seen many of these people for many years and felt very safe to show my emotions, which I was grateful for, because I could not hold them back.

After taking people through a healing meditation, I always open up to questions and answers from Spirit. People ask personal questions, and Spirit answers them through me.

A woman in the audience shared that her husband had passed away about two months ago and she wanted to know if her three children would be okay. Our hearts met in raw, vulnerable, pain as her husband answered through me. He was giving me information to give to her.

She said one of their issues when he was alive was that he didn't believe in the Spiritual world and was against her healing or awakening spiritually and certainly against mediums. He didn't believe in it.

I said, "Well, he believes in it now! He is in Spirit and is communicating to you through me." You are talking to a medium. He shared that it was his time to go and that he is around the kids and they feel him around them. She nodded! She had felt totally disconnected from him and was afraid to open up spiritually because he was very much against it.

Later after the evening was over, she told a friend that on the way home that night she could feel him with her, and they were on the same team again.

The next morning, he came to me and thanked me. He said on the Earth he had many opinions and he was not always easy to deal with because he was sometimes pig-headed. I had to laugh because we were both surprised that he used the term pig-headed. We both knew this was not something he would usually say.

He wanted me to give her the message and to also tell her that of course the kids would be fine, that she was such a great mother and also that he would be with her and the kids. She was very grateful. She felt like she was with her husband again.

I was going over our conversation and thinking about the word medium. It is not usually a title or word that I use to describe myself. I felt like that had come through me from Spirit to tell me that I am a medium.

When people ask me what kind of spiritual work I do, I sometimes have a hard time describing it. My connection to Spirit has always been part of me. I haven't taken classes to learn; I have always had the gift. When I was young, I just thought that everyone communicated with Spirit the same way I did. Communicating with the Spirit world was always easy for me; I didn't have to learn it. Spirit was my foundation.

Communicating with my family unit and others on the Earth was more challenging for me to understand and to learn. Spirit was my world and safety.

In the morning after the woman's husband had communicated with me, I saw him sitting very peacefully looking out over dimensions of light. The way I could explain it would be like looking at a beautiful sunset of many colors, but the sunset looked like it expanded into many clouds; they just kept going on and the colors kept unfolding and opening up. There was no end to these dimensions ... there are no words.

He was so very peaceful looking out through dimensions of God, or Creator. I was smiling to myself. He sure does believe in Spirit now. As I was watching and experiencing his serenity, I saw Frank come and sit down next to him. They didn't really speak; they connected through the energy of God, of Knowingness. They were home together in love, peace, gratitude, and grace.

I could then feel Frank take in the beauty of the majestic moment. I had witnessed him look at the ocean on the Earth in the same way, in awe of the incredible beauty. The ocean was God, Creation, for him.

Although I didn't know this man while he was on the Earth, I felt his love and how much he was at peace with his environment. He was home and I was home with them in my heart. I felt like I was with both of my boys. I knew this more through my heart, through Frank's heart; we had merged into One heart of Love.

CHAPTER NINETEEN

Walking with Jesus

November 2018

I had a hard time sleeping, and I have been waking up early and have not been able to go back to sleep. I have also been staying up very late, not because I have been interested in anything. I have been watching TV, just flipping channels just to pass the time.

This morning when I woke up early, I decided to meditate Ma Ma Ma as Mother Mary has taught me. I don't know how long I had been meditating, but I felt my heart start to open and felt a breath of life start to fill my whole body.

Then my man Jesus appeared and wanted me to walk with Him. I could also feel Frank with Him, but Jesus was guiding me and doing the talking.

He took me into the tunnel of light, the light that people who have gone through near death experiences (NDE) talk about when they return to the Earth. He wanted me to stay there with Him, to feel my body fill with love and peace, to experience myself leaving the consciousness of this earthly world.

As my body was filling with love and light, the frozen, painful emotions started breaking loose, and I started coughing uncontrollably. I could feel the pain and fear clearing out of my heart, chest and body. Jesus then said, "Stay here with Me." As I did, more of the old congestion continued to dissipate, and I became peaceful and calm in a cloud of love.

From that place of grace, I felt what seemed like I was asleep, but I was in a very alive dream with Jesus and Frank. My whole spiritual team was there, and we were very happy, laughing and talking about the book and the spiritual work that Frank would be assisting me with.

I know I was gone for quite some time. When Jesus asked me to walk with him, it was around 6:00am, and when I awoke it was 11:00am. I was very surprised at how much time had passed.

When I woke up, my body felt light and free. I no longer felt sick, and I had energy to get up and function.

As I looked around my room, everything looked very bright, beautiful and alive. My house felt clean. I felt like the healing I was taken through also cleared my house from my depression, hopelessness, my sickness, etc.

Before this experience, I was lying in the bed thinking I should start listening to music again, but I thought I didn't really have the energy and knew how much Frank loved music, and I was afraid I would feel too much pain from the memories.

Now I feel like listening to Christmas music. I had been afraid to because it would remind me of Frank. Elvis Christmas album was Frank's favorite album of all time. I always laughed about that because when I was pregnant with Frank, throughout the Christmas season, I listened to Elvis Christmas album over and over.

When Frank listened to it, he must have had a memory of being in the womb and Elvis Christmas songs must have brought back the memories and some kind of comfort.

Throughout my whole grief/rebirth experience, I am very aware that I am experiencing what I teach. Unexpressed feelings and emotions, old memories that need to be forgiven, block our own self-love, self-worth, and create sickness and disease.

I have always taught from my own healing experiences, but this is definitely the hardest and yet most profound experience and awakening of my life.

November 28, 2018
Colleen Leaves This World

Frank has been with me and has asked me to call his daughter, Danilla, which I agreed to do but, I haven't been able to reach out to her. I have felt frozen in fear and have been very aware that I don't want to feel the pain, the loss of him on the level that I did when he first left.

She is only 12 years old and I know she is having a hard time without her daddy. I am also aware that my emotions are frozen from fear of feeling the depth of loss that she must be feeling.

I have felt guilty for not calling her and because of the emotional, frozen guilt have not been able to connect with Frank as easily as I had been.

I received a call from my oldest friend, Colleen, who was supposed to come for Christmas and stay for a few months. I was very excited that she would be with me.

She called to let me know that she would not be coming because she had been diagnosed with cancer. She had been given six months to a year if she didn't go through chemo, conventional cancer healing. If she went through chemo, maybe two to six years. I was stunned. I could not actually hear what she was saying to me.

I called her back yesterday to hear what the diagnosis had been. Colleen and her husband Larry had been with me when I started my spiritual journey. Many years ago, I was teaching classes every week and they were always there. We became family with each other. They were my oldest, spiritual family and friends. I felt like my whole foundation was being taken from me, shattered.

Colleen had decided not to do chemotherapy. Her husband Larry had died two years prior to Colleen's receiving her diagnosis and she had seen what the chemo had done to his body. She didn't want to go through that.

Colleen had a very strong faith. She was everyone's cheerleader. Even with her diagnosis, she was still her positive, jovial self. She was comforting me and her whole family. Once she decided she was going to go home to be with Jesus and her husband, she left three months later in love and gratitude from her earthly life.

I am amazed how our emotions shift and change from one moment to the next. Some days, many days, I feel incredible having Frank with me from the other side, and the next day, I move back into grief, loss, separation and despair. It is also interesting to watch and see what triggers the different emotions.

But... as I continue to move through the different layers and cycles of the emotions, I definitely experience myself much lighter, happier, and my heart is much more open to people in love, appreciation and gratitude.

December 4, 2018

I was decorating my house for Christmas and the first thing I always put up is my angel made out of paper mache` that Frank made for me when he was in 4th grade. It is my favorite Christmas piece.

After I put it up, I would always call Frank to let him know his angel is up and is now bringing his light and love into my home. Even as an adult, he always seemed so proud that he was honored. I can still feel and hear his chuckle.

When I put his angel out this year, I cried. I could feel Frank's energy with me laughing like he always did.

The grief comes but now does not last as long. Grief, loss, feels like it is its own entity, its own person, has its own consciousness and it surfaces when I least expect it.

But, my love for Frank and my ability to connect with Frank has now become stronger than the grief; the grief will not win.

I am very grateful that I had Frank for as many years that we shared together. He was and is a beautiful Soul who loved life, people, the Earth, nature and the ocean.

Later today, I went to see a woman who does bodywork: cranial-sacral work. She is visiting Sedona from California.

I have been feeling pretty good lately and am surprised myself that I am having so many good days. I hear myself laughing again and feel joyful.

The grief still comes out at unexpected moments, like when I hear a song or someone says something that reminds me of Frank or even a scent or the sunset. It is really interesting when the grief comes up, but now it does not stay as long.

When I walked into the room to have a session with the woman who does cranial sacral therapy, the grief immediately surfaced. She said that whatever is stored in the body will surface to release or clear out.

I shared with her about Frank leaving this year. We both felt Frank immediately come into the room. She said he is standing to my right, which is where he always stands next to me. Nancy said he is so pure, his heart, his love. He doesn't even have a piece of lint on him; he is so pure.

Then he started expanding beyond the Earth and was showing her the Spirit world. She said, "Oh my God. He is such a high spiritual Being. He is working multidimensionally."

I replied, "Yes. He is." She responded that now Jesus is with Frank. They are really close, great friends. I said, "Yep. They are buddies."

Frank continued to expand himself and show her the Spirit world, many different dimensions, all the while talking to her and explaining the spiritual work that he and I will be doing together. He was grateful she was helping me to heal my body. He was so light, happy and joyful.

Nancy is a very serious woman and at one point, he even laughed and told her to lighten up and not take things so seriously. He then did Shaka.*

*Shaka means hang loose, chill out, a Hawaiian expression.

Nancy then said, "He is so gorgeous. Oh my God, he is gorgeous. Wow, he is beautiful, gorgeous inside and out." I explained that he was very handsome and when he was about 18 years old, the girls at one of his favorite surfing spots started calling him Monk the Hunk! His last name was Monk, so Monk the Hunk was his nickname or just The Hunk. We continued to call him that for the rest of his life.

When he was diagnosed with kidney and heart failure eight years prior to his death, he was still Monk the Hunk.

The following year after his diagnosis, while visiting Hawaii, my sister and I were meeting Frank and my Granddaughter, Danilla, for dinner. Danilla came running up to me and Frank was behind her. I absolutely did not recognize him. His body had deteriorated, and he looked like a little, old man; I was shocked and felt heartbroken.

Throughout dinner I kept staring at him and wanted to cry but held it back and remained focused on the love that we had with each other. I wondered how he felt when he looked in the mirror. I explained this to Nancy and Frank laughed. He said he needed to close down his body or good looks so that he could focus on healing emotionally and awakening spiritually.

I took a deep breath and let go of my emotional pain that I had carried around since Frank got sick. Now, of course, this made sense to me. Frank never ever complained about being sick. As I mentioned before, he had shared with me while he was

SURFING THROUGH HEAVEN'S DOORWAYS

alive that if he had not gotten sick, he would not have grown spiritually on the level that he had.

God, Jesus, love, forgiveness, compassion was Frank. It is who he was and is, not through a church or religion but from his spiritual connection to God, Jesus and the Source.

When Nancy and I finished our session, I felt like I could float off the table; Much of the pain my body had been carrying was gone. I felt flexible, very light and free.

I have made a very conscious effort to start healing my body. It is amazing what grief, loss, does to the physical body. I have been very weak. Last year, my body was strong from yoga and working out, and my intention now is to bring my body's mental, emotional and physical strength and health back.

The next day when I saw Nancy, she was laughing about her experience with Frank. She said he was so light and gorgeous and that she felt like a 16-year-old again in his energy. We both laughed. That was certainly the effect that he had on people, on women.

CHAPTER TWENTY

Healing Past Memories /
Returning to Love

December 14, 2018

I awoke this morning with what I call the holy light coming into my body.

A couple of days ago, I had the best day since Frank's departure from the Earth. I felt happy, joyful and had energy to start returning people's calls. I started reaching out to people who I love, also to my Facebook friends from all over the world who loved and supported me, and to my spiritual family that held me, loved me and totally embraced me in love after Frank left. I really don't know how I would have gotten through this without the unconditional love and support that I have received. People actually held me, hugged me as I cried. Some even cried together with me.

The next day after my happy day, I seemed to bottom out again as the grief once again slipped in through old, hurtful guilt-filled emotions. The beautiful light had once again activated a level of old energy that needed to be cleared out, so I could awaken and download more of my light. We cannot put the new on top of the old. The more we clear out old, emotional energies, the more room we have to integrate with the higher aspects of ourselves.

I was watching a program where a woman just put her busy schedule aside to hold her baby that was probably a few months old. I started thinking of Frank when he was a baby. I really can't remember holding him much. As a baby Frank was sick and cried a lot. I remember taking him to the doctor often, trying to figure out what was wrong.

His father and I were separated. I was 18 when Frank was born, and he was my second child. I had my first when I was 16. His father and I separated when I was pregnant: 17 and expecting my second child and I really did not want another child.

I remember my aunt Cecile, who was the pillar of love and support for me, really wanted me to give the baby that I was carrying up for adoption.

Although I did not want another baby, I could not even conceive of the idea of giving the baby away. And … I am so grateful that I didn't. Frank was one of the greatest gifts and lights of my life. He was such a beautiful, loving, sensitive little boy and man.

When Frank was a little boy and heard my car pull up as I got home from work, he would come running out the door yelling and excited. "Mom's home!" He would always help me carry groceries in the house. He was such a gentle, loving Being even as a little boy.

When Frank was under a year old, we were at the doctor's office again, and the doctor finally said, "I don't know what is wrong with this child." We had been at the doctors many times Frank's first year. He then said, "I think he is retarded." (In those days retarded is what they used to call people who were challenged.). "He has a retarded look. His tongue hangs out like a retarded person." He said that he wanted me to get a second opinion and sent me to a specialist.

I was in shock and felt heartbroken. Since Frank's father, Phil, and I had split up, I had not really been connecting with God. It was the first time in my life that God, Jesus and Spirit had not been my conscious safety and guiding light. Unconsciously, I knew that they were still guiding me. I could not have gotten through my challenging childhood without Jesus holding my hand and walking with me.

But when Phil left me when I was pregnant with Frank, I was heartbroken and felt let down by God. So, for about a year, I had closed down my communication with God. I was young and felt let down and abandoned by God. Of course, as I have matured, my understanding of God and Source has certainly shifted and expanded.

So, here I was, 18 years old in a doctor's office with my second child and the doctor was telling me my child was retarded. I can still remember the feeling that I felt back then; I felt so alone with nowhere to turn, no one to help me.

I cried all the way home, sobbed at the same time, praying and talking to God, like I had never before. I cried all night actually begging God; I guess I was negotiating. "Please take my arms, legs, whatever you want from me. Please do it to me, not my son. Please, please heal my son."

I remember so vividly my feelings and emotions as the new doctor was examining Frank. I was frozen in fear. The doctor starts laughing and says as he is looking down Frank's throat, that there is nothing wrong with this kid. He can't breathe. His tonsils are so big, and you can actually see his adenoids by looking down his throat.

So, at one year old, Frank had his tonsils and adenoids taken out. As soon as I brought him home from the hospital, he jumped on his rocking horse (that he had not been on before) and was rocking for lost time. Having his tonsils and adenoids taken out gave him lifeforce. He had energy to function, and he rocked for the rest of his life. His surfboard was his rocking horse.

As I was watching this woman on TV make the decision to hold her child instead of being on the computer and getting busy with life, my memories, pain and guilt, surfaced for not holding Frank when he was a baby. Of course, I held him when he cried, fed him and took care of his needs, but I couldn't remember holding him in love. Our beginning life together had been pretty much survival. I remember the moment that I bonded with him. He was a little over one-year-old.

I would love to be able to hold my precious little boy and let him know how much I loved him.

Bonding with Frank

I remember the exact moment I bonded with Frank. He was actually about 1 ½ years old, and I was 19 years old. I was with my boyfriend at the time. He was driving, and I was holding Frank up against me. I was holding the front of him, his heart up against mine. In those days, we didn't have seat belts.

I felt Frank's love come into me, heart to heart. It was not a jolt of love; it was like the light and love from his heart came into mine and filled me up with a warmth that I had never experienced before. I felt like peace, love and innocence was filling up my whole body.

The whole front of my body filled up first. This love with Frank moved from my heart up into my throat, into my arms, then moved down into my intestines and into my legs and feet. The love then moved into the back of my body, into my spine, my nervous system, my sacrum, up into my neck, and into my head.

My cells started tingling with light and the warmth, and safety of love filled my whole body. I felt home in love. My cells merged with his. We became One heart of Love.

I had merged in love with my beautiful boy. Our Souls had reconnected in love as One Soul.

From that moment forward, our hearts were One heart. Frank and I were very close. During the most difficult, challenging times of my life, Frank was always there for me, as I was always there for him.

He turned light and love on for me. As I write this, I can feel the experience of that moment.

When my first child, Tricia, was born, I was 16 and desperately wanted love. I needed love. I remembered holding her, and I could not believe that she was mine, that I had made her. That she had grown inside of me. That was the first moment I really understood love.

For the first six months of Tricia's life, all I wanted to do was hold her close and protect her. I think I was giving her the love, safety and protection that I had needed and didn't get. I remember my apartment being a mess, but I didn't care. All I wanted to do was hold my daughter, my bundle of love.

Unfortunately, when Frank was born, the circumstances were very different. I was alone at 18 and expecting my second child.

As I look back and feel the moment that I first bonded Frank, my heart and body is again filling up with the same love and Oneness.

As I am writing, Frank from the Spirit world is sitting next to me on the couch. He also is going back to the moment that we actually turned the light and love on for each other. He has a beautiful smile on his face and is permeating love.

Our third eyes are the higher eye of Creation. As we look into each other's eyes, we move beyond time and expand multidimensionally into One heart of Love.

Then he laughs. He is very humorous and once again sends me the song "One Love" by Bob Marley. I laugh with him.

God, I am so grateful to have this connection with him from the dimensions beyond this world. Thank you.

I cried all day just like I had many years ago when the doctor told me that Frank was retarded, only this time for the loss of those precious moments and experiences.

I went from feeling very high and happy the day before into a grief and loss for a couple of days that I could not seem to come out of. I felt like a zombie walking through life. I watched TV night and day not even knowing what I was watching. I wanted something to focus on to take the pain away.

I decided to have some wine thinking that would help. At 2:00 in the morning, I was still watching TV, nothingness. I was surprised when I woke up yesterday in my bed and fully clothed. I don't remember getting up and going into bed.

Finally, yesterday morning I called on Jesus to help me please. In desperation, I begged Jesus to help me come out of this grief and depression.

Jesus came to me and asked me to walk with Him as He had done so many times before in my life. I said, "Hold my hand so I can feel you with me, so I feel safe." I could feel my hand in His. He was very strong and yet so loving. He took me through dimensions and into the place where Mother Mary had taken me.

I once again saw the Souls that were getting ready to come to the Earth. The Souls that would come as children who are being born totally conscious. They were in the big, outdoor arena that I had seen before. As I looked over to the right, I once again saw Frank teaching and sharing his knowledge of the Earth — what was happening here and what people would/could expect as they came down here.

Those Souls would be coming down totally conscious, remembering who they are spiritually, and they needed to have a larger picture of what their Soul, Spirit, was coming into.

When Frank saw me standing there, his eyes lit up and with a big smile on his face, he said, "Hey, Mama." His heart opened up to me. He was very happy to see me and brought me to the center of the stage and introduced me to his audience.

He shared with them that he would not have been able to grow spiritually on the level that he had without me. He said I continuously opened more doors for him to move through spiritually. The DNA cleansing, clearing and healing, and the Soul retrieval that I was continuing to do, cleared the patterns and programs out of him and our ancestors backwards and forwards.

As this happened, it cleared him out of old, karmic ancestral patterns and opened up his light Creator/Spirit/Christ/I AM DNA systems.

I was very grateful to be with Frank again, to hear his laugh and experience his joy of life.

He was coming to an end of his teachings and as I stood there with him, I could feel a beautiful light, love, continue to fill me up and start to clear the painful emotions out of my body. My whole right side (my male side) kept filling with this light love. Then my left side (my feminine side) also started filling with love.

I felt like I could breathe again.

As people started clearing out of the arena, Frank wanted me to walk with him. He was very joyful, happy and peaceful. He was doing his spiritual work and was at peace with everyone and everything.

We were walking down a crystal walkway with beautiful columns of light on both sides of the walkways.

I was asking Frank to forgive me for not being present with him when he was a baby. He laughed and said, "Mom, you were 18 years old."

We continued to walk down the crystal walkway and came to a beautiful garden where I saw many people, Souls, gathered together. People were laughing and sharing with each other. They were dressed in many beautiful colors of pastels and their joy and laughter expanded into beautiful music.

We walked to an arena that overlooked the garden, and I saw beautiful colors in the clouds, like amazingly breathtaking sunsets or sunrises.

Frank explained as the Creator had, that all Souls have their own unique tone or sound and when these tones come together, they create a symphony of sound. Each sound has a color, and when Souls come together in this way, their collective sound creates the beautiful colors through all dimensions. They created the colors that I am experiencing multidimensionally. These are also the frequencies and colors that many artists on the Earth plane are now bringing through in their paintings and artwork.

We continued to walk down the crystal walkway with the great pillars of light on both sides. The pillars were crystal and emanated beautiful colors like when the sun hits a crystal and rainbows of color come into a room.

We came to a huge illuminated building and Frank showed me that it was a library, a record room, just like on the Earth. We have libraries of our history. I asked what the record room was for and how it was different from the Akashic records.

He explained that the Akashic records are our Soul's record of every lifetime, memory and experience a Soul has ever gone through or experienced.

The record room holds every experience that our planet has ever gone through; every civilization, the different cycles of the Earth, and the different timelines of the Earth are stored in this record room. How the Earth had been cleared of the civilizations for the next story, or agreement, that needed to be experienced and played out on the Earth, is also stored in this record room.

These records are open to anyone in the Spirit world. As Souls go into this record room, they can follow their Soul's genetic coding, DNA of their earthly journey. They can trace their history all the way through Earth's timelines and into other timelines on other planets, and of course, dimensions.

He explained that we each have our own Soul's journey and that there is also a collective Souls' journey, or DNA system, and as we look at this DNA system, we can choose which system, or what we call bloodline, we want to reincarnate through.

Each system has a frequency and as we look at our own Akashic records journal, we can see what lessons our own Soul is still needing to complete.

We then choose which frequency, or collective bloodline, we will incarnate through.

Every bloodline has its own sound tone, frequency. When we are getting ready to come to the Earth or another planet, we will move into the realm that carries that frequency.

If we choose to come to the Earth and experience our self in a Jewish religion, we will come together with others in the like frequency. The same is true for Mormons, Catholics, Christians, Muslims and other religions.

You will gather together in an energy space or dimension and wait for your exact number to be called: the number being the exact astrological number, frequency, that will set up your whole life's pattern and journey.

Spirit has shown me in my sessions with others that you come to the Earth with your Soul's karmic agreements, contracts, and the genetic make-up from your parents and ancestors. Your Soul's agreement and purpose is to move beyond, or transcend, these agreements and contracts. As you do, you merge into the higher aspects of yourself, becoming one with Spirit in your physical body, to live from your higher self's consciousness, to co-create Heaven on Earth now, to not wait until we are in Spirit to remember who we are.

CHAPTER TWENTY-ONE

My First Christmas Without Frank

December 24, 2018

My first Christmas without Frank was very challenging. I was not going to decorate, but my sister was coming from Hawaii to spend Christmas with me, so I felt like I needed to put some decorations up.

Christmas time for me, my family and my children, has always been very special. Christmas has always been my favorite time of year.

Whatever was going on in my dysfunctional childhood always came to a halt at Christmas. We always had beautiful, loving, family Christmases.

As I said, my parents met the night my father got back from the war and without help to heal his condition, he was an emotional mess, as was my childhood.

As a child, we moved every year, sometimes two times a year. I went to a new school every year, sometimes two schools in a year.

My father drank heavily and when drunk was very violent towards my mother. The police had been called to our house numerous times.

After one of his episodes, he would disappear. When he returned feeling guilty, ashamed and confused, he would want to start over, a new start for our family, so we would move for a new beginning.

But...whatever was going on between my parents or if my father was gone somewhere, he would always come home for Christmas, usually with great gifts for all of us.

We always had great Christmases with extended family. This was like declaring a truce for Christmas.

I carried this tradition into my family with my children. We always had big, extended family, heartfelt, loving Christmases.

I moved to Hawaii when my children were young. I was going through a challenging divorce and felt like one of us needed to make a move. So I did, and it was the best decision I had ever made. Hawaii was our heart and home, our new life, and new beginning. At Christmas and on other holidays, we always opened our home and hearts to everyone. We had people from all over the world joining us; all were welcome.

So here I was, my first Christmas without Frank. I am very grateful that my sister is here with me.

I have white Christmas lights out on my porch, which is like an extended room, but this year I didn't feel like turning them on.

My sister stayed until New Year's Day, and as she was getting ready to leave, she was standing in my kitchen and could see the white lights on my porch had been turned on.

She said she must have accidentally turned the lights on when she was bringing firewood in, I explained there was no way the lights could have accidentally been turned on. You have to bend way down and turn on a switch. At that moment, I could feel Frank behind her laughing. He wanted to make sure that we knew he was with us, maybe not physically, but certainly spiritually. The next day the light came on again, and Frank was standing behind me laughing. He continually lets us know he is around.

CHAPTER TWENTY-TWO
My Best Friend Diana Passes

January 21, 2019

My oldest, best friend, Diana, passed to other dimensions this morning, January 21, 2019. It is only nine months after Frank made his transition. Once again, I am experiencing so much grief, loss, and heartbreak.

Diana had been my best friend for years. People used to say we were bonded at the hip. We were always together.

When I lived in Hawaii, I met Diana at a monthly group called Powerful Women.

I spoke, and when she heard what my profession was, she called me for a session. We immediately became best friends. She actually became my marketing manager. She was very intelligent. She had been a teacher, had written textbooks and was already a marketing manager for Junior Achievement. She was also very spiritual.

All of my life, I had felt stupid; I was dyslexic but didn't have a clue as to why I had a hard time learning. Back in the day, not much was known about dyslexia.

When I met Diana, she turned that around for me. I remember her saying, "Oh my God, Michelle. The higher intelligence that you have is what everyone wants. Many of us are intelligent from book learning, but you have a direct connection to the Source, the higher intelligence."

Diana knew how my brain worked and never, ever judged me. I never felt stupid or afraid of trying something, like putting flyers together, etc.

She honored me and helped me to see and feel my intelligence.

She helped me to learn. We worked very well together.

Diana's family and my family became an extended family. We shared all holidays together. We were one family and shared so much fun, joy, and happiness together Frank had actually taken Diana's daughter to the senior prom.

Diana was very connected to the angelic realms. Just as Jesus was my main man, the angels were Diana's strongest connection to the Spirit world. At one time, there was a big article in the newspaper about her. She was the angel lady of Hawaii. She was assisting others to heal through her connection to the Christ, angelic, realms.

Diana was also an ordained minister and officiated both Frank's and my daughter Jennifer's wedding.

I used to teach weekly classes, and in one of my classes, Spirit gave her the 23rd psalm. They said in days to come she would need it.

A few weeks later, Diana was diagnosed with stage 4 ovarian cancer and was given a 20% chance to live. I was at the hospital when she came out of surgery and received the news.

Diana's children were young, and she said she wanted to live long enough to see them graduate from high school. I started giving Diana healing sessions, and Spirit guided her step-by-step out of cancer. We went into any past life we could find when she had been sick, hurt, or powerless in any way.

I found a beautiful hilltop home for her to rent, while she was still in the hospital. This allowed her to leave a toxic relationship. When she left the hospital, she moved into her new home.

Diana had her first round of chemo, and after the first round, Spirit told her she was done with cancer. When she refused to have another round of chemo, the doctors said she needed surgery again. She refused. She really trusted the guidance that came through me. Like I said, we gave her many healing sessions.

We cleared past lives but also the patterns and hurts from her childhood and throughout this lifetime.

Diana was cancer-free for over 25 years. Diana was living a difficult, stressful life, and the cancer came back a few years ago. She left this world in January.

When Diana left nine months after Frank, I felt like I had lost my foundation. I could not even call her daughter. I was too heartbroken. I couldn't stop crying. Diana and I had the same spiritual consciousness. I could always call her when I didn't understand left brain thinking.

She would always very patiently walk me through whatever I need to understand.

While on the Earth together, Diana and Frank were very close When Diana left this world and went home into the Spirit world, I saw Frank waiting for her.

A few days after she left, I saw Frank playing his guitar, and Diana was with him. All of her loved ones were gathered around Frank, and they were laughing as he played and sang for them.

I will see you soon, Diana Jane, my beautiful Soul Sister. I am sure you are teaching others in the Spirit world and are hanging out with your beautiful angels.

Thank you for being my support, my teacher, and most of all, my friend. I love you, Michelle.

CHAPTER TWENTY-THREE

Back in Sweden / My Tour

April 1, 2019

After my two-day workshop in Skelleftea, Sweden, one year after Frank's departure from this world, I felt a peace within that I had never experienced before in life. I felt complete. As I looked over my life, I felt like it had been a life well lived. My life had been one of service, and I felt like my spiritual work had assisted many others to heal, to clear out ancestral, karmic patterns.

I felt like I was done, not in a negative way. I didn't feel depressed or suicidal like I had the previous year; I felt at peace with myself, my life, and everyone.

This must have been what Frank felt or was talking about when he was sharing, reviewing, his life with me before he left.

I felt like I had completed my journey on Earth and was at peace and felt satisfied with all of it.

The interesting part is that during the workshop I had just facilitated, I had been taken into a realm, a dimension, and I was in front of the karmic board where I felt love, joy, laughter, and satisfaction. I signed another contract, or commitment, to stay on the Earth until my sister, Melody, leaves. When she leaves the Earth, I can then follow her into the Spirit world.

I feel fine with that. Whether I stay or leave, I feel very peaceful. Because I work in the Spiritual world much of the time, I am very comfortable there and now feel very at ease on the Earth.

As I said before, like many of you, my earthly journey has not been easy. We signed up for completion in this lifetime. The Creator talks about this lifetime being the one of completion, that nothing you have gone through is new. Everything has a frame of reference someplace else, meaning other lifetimes or dimensions. We are here to clear out the old, karmic agreements and contracts to make room for us to ascend into the higher dimensions of ourselves. Because we are really ONE in higher dimensions, as we clear out old DNA, ancestral patterns, we heal it for our past and future generations.

When we are in the Spirit world and setting our intentions for our earthly lifetime, we forget what it is like emotionally to go through the lessons.

When we get to Earth, we have amnesia. As we go through clearing our Soul's agreed upon assignments, we heal and clear old, karmic agreements and emotions. From this healing, we start awakening and remembering our higher light and purpose.

After the workshop, I felt like all of the emotional stories had lifted, and I felt free, pretty neutral to all of it.

As I lay in the bed the morning after making my connection to God, Creator and my spiritual team, I felt myself drifting beyond any time frequency and into a dimension of light. I realized I was in the animal kingdom. I could see my two cats, Princess and Elvis that I had loved so much. I felt love and joy with them, a homecoming. As I was continuing to move through this dimension, I saw and moved through a light doorway. The door was multidimensional and expanded through all timelines. As I moved through the doorway, more timelines kept opening and the doorway became many doorways continuing to open and expand.

I was moving very quickly through timelines of light, and I could not see anyone around me. And yet, I knew I was not alone. I was everyone and everything. As I cleared the timelines, I ended in a dimension of all knowing. I could not see the Earth, but I knew all of Earth's history in a moment of time.

Although I had heard and knew in my head that all except

love is an illusion, I was now experiencing that all is an illusion.

The Spirit world of love and Oneness is our Soul's true essence; it is real, and the Earth's consciousness and all that we go through is the illusion

We have it in reverse. I hear people say "in the real world" meaning Earth's world, and it is actually the opposite: the "real world" is Spirit, and the earthly is the illusion.

When I came back from the experience into my physical body, I felt very clear, clean, and still. I was vibrating in the Isness of God's love, in the Christ love, into that which we are collectively shifting. We are remembering who we are. We are Spirit having a human experience not the other way around.

As I looked around the room, everything looked different in the world of matter. When I got up, I touched the physical furniture in my room. What a contrast.

That day I was actually flying back to Stockholm, Sweden. While at the airport, I could feel that everyone around me was me. We were all Cells of the One higher consciousness.

The following week, April 13, would be the one-year anniversary of Frank leaving the Earth into the Spirit world. A part of me thinks I should feel the loss and grief that has plagued me so much of this last year, and yet, I feel so peaceful and euphoric.

CHAPTER TWENTY-FOUR

One Year Anniversary of Frank Leaving

April 13, 2019

This is the day one year ago that Frank made his transition into the Spirit world.

Although I have had so many miraculous experiences since he left, as the day was nearing, I was feeling apprehension. I did not want to feel the horrific pain and loss that I had felt last year.

I awoke early in the morning with Frank in the room with me. My room was lit up with light, and Frank was so joyous and happy. All I could feel was love, joy, and a great peace and sense of freedom where no boundaries existed.

The love, light, was filling me up and my cells and whole body were tingling beyond my physical body. Once again, I felt the freedom of not being in a physical body. I was one with all consciousness.

Frank asked me to walk with him, and we walked together beyond time and shifted into the peaceful, colorful realms of the Spirit world. The peace and love is beyond anything that can be explained.

We walked through the beautiful crystal colonies of light and down a garden pathway, glided up a hill that overlooked vibrating crystal fields.

The colors were magnificent, like watching crystal sunrises and sunsets at the same time. All of the colors blending together created a harmonic resonance beyond anything I have ever heard or can compare.

We sat together at a table and chairs overlooking the crystal fields and meadows. The colors kept flowing together creating beautiful music. The music's frequency was very subtle and healing.

I was so grateful to be sitting with my beautiful son and talking with him as we did while he was on the Earth. The difference being that he is truly a very evolved teacher and healer. He was always love and compassion while he was on the Earth, but his arena is now huge.

He showed me that this is one of his favorite places that he comes to be at one with God-Spirit. When he spends time here, he expands beyond any of his teaching roles and agreements back into the Oneness of silence — Source.

I asked how he could be in so many places at one time, with me, his sister, his daughter Danilla, Monica and in so many others. I also asked how Jesus could be in so many millions of places at once answering so many prayers and communicating with many at the same time. Frank explained the collective consciousness.

As we sat there together, I started becoming very peaceful and tired. The frequency vibration was so much higher than I was used to experiencing. I told him I needed to come back into my room and sleep. I drifted back to sleep full of light, love and peace beyond any energy I had ever experienced before.

Later when I awoke, all I could feel was deep peace, love, and gratitude.

What a gift to be able to connect with my son on this level, beyond any earthly story. He amazes me. He is such a beautiful light Being and is now my teacher and guide from the other side. I am learning so much and am very grateful to be able to share my experience with many on the Earth, to assist all of us into another level of our Soul's awakening.

Later that day, my friend Judith and I went to a concert at a gorgeous, old church. The church's name is Sophia. So perfect. The Creator explains his feminine heart or the feminine of creation is Sophia. Today was an amazing full circle experience. So grateful. Thank you, God — Creator. Thank you, Frank.

When I returned to Sweden in April 2019, I was speaking to a group and a woman came up to me afterwards and said that as soon as she walked into the room, she could feel Frank's presence. Two other women came up to me afterwards and confirmed that they also had seen and felt Frank with them. It is very heartwarming to know that others also experience his presence. It is definitely confirmation for me.

While I was working in a clinic doing private sessions, I felt like I wanted to open a window for fresh air, but the top window (the one that could open) was so high up that I would have to get a chair to try to open it. I didn't know if I would be able to close it again. Because of that, I did not open it.

The next day while at the clinic, the owner asked me if I had opened the top window because when she came in the morning, the window was wide open. Frank had great humor while on the Earth, and he still sees and does things that are pretty funny. He was letting me know that he was with me.

I had put a healthy bar in my purse because I was going to be on a long train ride. When I went to eat it, it had already been opened. It was obvious that someone had opened it. Frank was helping me again.

Frank Explaining Collective Consciousness

We are multidimensional Beings. There may be times on the Earth when you will have a thought of someone, and they call you or you end up seeing them or running into them.

Thought is energy. Perhaps they were thinking of you and you picked up on their thought. Your thought then came together with theirs and opened a line of communication. You became one thought beyond time.

In the higher Spiritual realms, you are expanded through all consciousness, past, present and future. Any relationship you have had with someone is still in your memory bank, your subconsciousness mind.

You are actually communicating from your higher self's energy. This energy is multidimensional and has no limitation or time.

Remember, we are actually One Soul, or cell, that has split into many different personalities. As we move from our earthly frequencies, we shift back into the One Soul. Because we are not separate, we can communicate with everyone at the same time.

Imagine yourself taking a live, computer class. The instructor is teaching live, and many of you are on the line. The teacher is explaining what many of you are wanting to understand. Then the teacher opens the call up for people to ask personal questions, and he answers each question individually.

In the higher realms, we can answer everyone's personal questions all at once, at the same time. We can do this because we are not communicating from a timeline. We are communicating from the collective consciousness of our One Being.

Souls are multidimensional Beings. We have no restriction of time and because of this, we can be every place at once.

When I am assisting you in your workshops, I am an expanded consciousness and can assist to heal everyone at the same time. You are actually doing the same thing. When you take people through a healing meditation, you are assisting everyone at the same time.

The higher the vibration of a Soul, the more expanded their consciousness is. Their expanded consciousness can reach more people at the same time.

Jesus is the OverSoul for the Souls on planet Earth. He is the Christ awakening for our planet. Because of this, he is able to connect with everyone at once

He is the Creator energy that is expressing itself in form. Even though he is no longer on the Earth in form, the memory of his form still exists there. He is the link between Heaven and Earth.

Because we are a collective consciousness, Jesus is able to respond, answer everyone's prayers at the same time.

This is also the same for other religions and belief systems. Buddha, Krishna, Baba Ji, etc. and other higher Beings of light, Masters and Angels are the link between the earthly consciousness and the Source of Creation.

The Creator's energy is a raw, pure Source energy, an omnipresence, infinite intelligence, of love, of Creation.

This intelligence is waiting to serve you in the highest, or in whatever your consciousness is. Whatever you put out to the Universe, or Creation, will come back to you tenfold.

The Creator and all of the higher Beings are the support system of Creation itself. This intelligence is constantly expanding into a higher knowing as we are.

We are the cells, the Souls, of Creator, of God, of the supreme Beingness.

We are ascending and all timelines are crashing and blending together into One consciousness. This One consciousness is the higher heart and mind of God, Source, Creator.

We are coming home together into the heart of One Love, in our physical bodies now. We are awakening into the infinite intelligence within ourselves and living from our higher consciousness. This is Ascension.

CHAPTER TWENTY-FIVE

Easter Sunday / My Five-Day Workshop

April 21, 2019

For years during Easter, I have facilitated a five-day workshop in Sweden. I love facilitating this five-day workshop. Because of the circumstances last year, with Frank leaving, the workshop was cancelled. One of the women, Cecelia, who had signed up for the workshop was very disappointed. She wanted me to come to her home the next year, 2019, and do my five-day workshop. She would set everything up and all I would have to do is show up. She lives on a very magical, creative island by the name of O'land and has a beautiful healing center there.

Cecelia is an incredible artist and author. Because artists of so many different venues live there, the island's energy is very light, creative, and freeing. Artists seem to dance to the beat of their own creative drum or juices. The workshop was the highest energy that has ever come through me. The whole group shifted and cleared many of their ancestral patterns and programs that they had become extensions of, and were playing out in this world. I know I keep repeating that each workshop is the highest, but as I am continuing to shift spiritually into higher dimensions, I am able to assist others to shift into higher dimensions of themselves.

As we clear the patterns out of our own DNA systems, it starts unraveling the patterns for future generations and past generations. As I expressed, I have found that there is usually one person in a family unit who is the light, the sensitive, who has agreed to go through much duality. As they start looking for ways to heal from their family pain, addictions, etc. the whole family starts healing and shifting. It is not an easy journey for the person or the family. This person is usually what is called the black sheep of the family, the one that has the most troubled life and as they go through life, the whole family is affected by the pain. Sometimes the black sheep may actually die from a drug overdose, in other ways, and even commit suicide.

Many times, from such an unimaginable loss and grief, the family's hearts start opening into a rebirth of what is important in life and the answer is always, always, love. Whatever the question, LOVE is always the answer.

In this workshop, people easily shifted out of their pain body into a higher knowing within themselves. I also feel that doing the five-day workshop over Easter is powerful because the Christ energy is so high. The death and rebirth of the Christ within us, the rebirth of love, compassion, acceptance and forgiveness.

I woke up Easter Sunday in love and gratitude for Jesus, his whole spiritual team, Magdalene, Archangel Michael and the other Archangels, Masters, and of course, my beautiful angel son, Frank.

I went to sleep the night before giving thanks in love and gratitude for being the link between Heaven and Earth. I am grateful to be able to bring so much healing to others from my own healing experiences. It is such a gift to bring Spirit's higher love and total acceptance through, so others feel safe enough to let go of past hurts, which allows them to open to receive love.

When I awoke Easter Sunday, my room was filled with what I call the "holy light of love, of God, of Creation." Frank was in the room smiling and so happy. Standing next to him was Jesus, my main man. Jesus was also emanating love and peace.

This morning, Jesus and Frank wanted me to walk with them. They took me to the same place that Frank had taken me on his first spiritual birthday.

We walked together through the beautiful crystal columns and on the path through the majestic live gardens. We kind of floated up the hill to the outlook where Frank and I had sat the morning of his one-year anniversary into the Spirit world and realms.

As I sat with them and we looked out at the majestic fields of color, the colors started shifting and fountains of colorful light started shooting up and out of the crystal. It almost looked like springtime with flowers opening up, popping open to share their beautiful colors and scents.

Jesus said that he and Frank share this time together often. This is a plateau where Masters, Angels, guides and teachers come to recharge their energy, to expand into the Isness.

I was feeling so honored that I was actually brought to this place, where Masters and Angels come and sit to balance themselves in the Oneness.

Then Jesus shared with me that the plateau where we are now sitting is an overlook of the Earth's awakening, or ascension. He said all of the lights that are coming on, or what I see as shooting out of the crystals, are all of the Beings (people) on Earth who are waking up and remembering who they are. The lights are people who are awakening spiritually and Soul groups that are coming back together. They are holding love and light for one another to come home inside of themselves as to what is important in life.

Afterwards, I lay in awe of what had been shown to me. Truly a rebirth, or ascension of a civilization, a consciousness on Earth, that was awakening into a higher awareness of what was important: love and compassion. We are shifting into our higher selves multidimensionally.

I was feeling pretty privileged that Jesus actually had me see and experience our evolution and ascension on Easter morning with my son Frank.

That day, Easter Sunday, I was taking people through a process and my two main men, Jesus and Frank, showed up and took the whole group through timelines, through the crystal columns and into their favorite spot overlooking our world. The whole group saw and experienced the awakening of our beautiful Mother Earth and all of us occupants.

I laughed hysterically with the group. So much for feeling very special. I was actually very grateful we all got to experience this together.

CHAPTER TWENTY-SIX

Jesus Healing Me

May 15, 2019

I have been doing many private sessions assisting people to clear old, emotional hurts, traumas and patterns from past experiences.

I was exhausted and I could hardly sleep. My body was in so much physical pain. My joints hurt and I ached all over. I was tossing and turning all night.

The next morning, Jesus came and wanted me to walk with him to our special place.

He explained that my body had absorbed the mental, emotional and physical pain that my clients had released, and I had taken it in as if it was my own. My etheric, energy body absorbed it.

He said it is very important that I clear my mental, emotional and physical bodies every day after working in people's energies. This is something I know and teach, and yet, I was too tired to clear myself.

The gift of the experience is such a great reminder of how we can take in, absorb, other people's energies and we become sick or ill because of it.

It's interesting because my third book *The Creator Heals* explains all of this. We always match and merge with our environment's energy. Our body takes it in and does not know that it is not ours. It becomes ours and short circuits our bodies.

When we understand this, we can choose what we want to match and merge with.

Jesus then assisted me. He cleared my bodies, and the pain was immediately gone.

After Jesus cleared other people's emotions from my body, he looked deeply into my eyes, Soul to Soul. His energy was very strong and pure, and as it started moving down and through my whole body, I felt very nauseated. His energy continued to clear old energy blocks, which moved my bodies back into balance.

After this healing and clearing, I was once again back in my body feeling very light, peaceful, and clear. I could feel my cells tingling in light and harmony.

May 16, 2019

I woke up with holy light coming in again. I was very tired and was trying to meditate and calm my body down, but it didn't seem to work. My man Jesus was there and asked me to walk with him to our special meeting place. As I sat there with him, I witnessed myself starting to chant "Jesus, Jesus, Jesus," which sent energy into my heart, and my body started filling with light and calmed down. I then automatically started chanting "Ma Ma Ma" for Mother Mary, and I started seeing and experiencing many beautiful pictures, scenes of festive energy and beautiful women throughout history. I automatically started chanting Jesus again, and my body was vibrating in great peace and balance with the male and female.

I was very surprised through this process that I had pictures of my Grandma Amy's funeral service. It was very real as if I was there going through the actual experience. I could see her very clearly, exactly what she looked like and what she was wearing. Her hands were folded very peacefully in front of her body.

My Grandma Amy died when I was 14 years old. She was my dad's mother, and she adored me. I was the light in her life.

I have an older brother, Mike, who has a different father than the other four of us. My Grandma Amy adored him until I was born. Then all of her attention went to me. As I started getting older, if I wanted a toy or something, my grandma would take it away from my brother and give it to me.

The behavior continued after my other siblings were born. If they had something and I wanted it, my grandmother would take it away from them and give it to me.

I was young and really didn't understand the behavior, but it created many issues towards me from my mother. My mother resented me for it. I do remember that when I was in the 4th grade my grandmother gave me a purple ten-speed bike for my birthday. The same year my grandmother gave my sister crayons, coloring books and scissors as a birthday present, and she gave me the same thing, only mine were nicer than my sister's.

My mother ended up hating my grandmother and continued to take her resentment out on me, blaming me for my grandmother's behavior.

As I was growing up, I started feeling guilty because my grandmother loved me and she did not show this love to my siblings.

When my grandmother died, I suppressed my grief and felt guilty that I was feeling such a loss that no one else other than my father was feeling.

Over the years I have thought about her dying and her funeral and could not remember any of it.

So, I was very surprised this morning when the healing from Jesus and Mother Mary unlocked the memories from my subconscious. Unlocking the memories also opened my heart to receive the great love and pride that my grandmother felt for me. I felt validated. I felt a warmth of love and the safety of love fill and permeate my whole body.

My inner children felt safe and loved.

A few years before my mother died (passed away), I was with her and she was once again going into a tirade about how much she hated Grandma Amy and all of the stories, unfairness, and invalidation that my siblings received from her.

As I was listening to my mother spew her hatred, I thought this is interesting. Everything that you feel Grandma Amy did to my brothers and sisters are the same things that you did to me.

My mother was constantly critical of everything I did and said: the way I dressed, my hair. I experienced her invalidation of me my whole life.

As I listened to my mother, I stopped her and said, "You know what, mom? I was just a little girl." My mother stopped and I knew she took it in. She had never thought of that before. I was just a child.

That was the last time I ever heard my mother project her hatred towards my grandma to me. She got it. I was just a child. It wasn't my fault.

I have been doing spiritual work for years and am still amazed at how much inside of us needs to surface to be healed. I am also surprised that as it clears how much freer we become to love and accept ourselves. We are able to experience our own value and self-worth as we move out of our ancestral patterns and projections of someone else's beliefs of who they think we are.

CHAPTER TWENTY-SEVEN

Back in Sedona / Crystal Generators

June 12, 2019

Frank has been around me all day wanting me to meditate and tune in. My intention was, and is, that when I return to Sedona, I would work on and finish our book.

After being gone for almost three months, I have been busy handling everything.

Finally, in the afternoon, I slowed down to meditate and was very quickly taken into the Spirit world. Jesus came and asked me to walk with him. He took me into a dimension of very large, huge crystals. It's hard to explain how large these crystals are. They are beyond anything you could even imagine on the Earth. I was in a dimension of crystal generators. All of the crystals emanated different colors and energy frequencies.

Jesus explained that each crystal held the energy of different planets that are in our solar system, universe and beyond. Many planets are so far away in other universes that they cannot be reached.

The crystals in this dimension hold the frequencies from the planets that are assisting our world, the Earth, through all ascension portals.

This dimension is a generator for all Beings on our planet that have reincarnated from other planets.

On our Soul's journey, we live many lifetimes, some on Earth and also lifetimes in other dimensions on other planets.

This dimension was like being in all consciousness at once.

It was certainly vibrating beyond the earthly energies of duality.

I felt like I was in a movie where one moves out of time and all worlds blend together as One consciousness of love, color and sound. As all blended together, a sense of complete silence vibrated through me where no time existed.

As I sat there with Jesus, old memories of this life started surfacing. I could see all of my life's patterns coming up and each memory of the patterns surfacing and leaving. There was no emotion connected to the patterns, but when they surfaced, I could feel my body becoming lighter and lighter. I could actually see patterns. They were many different shapes and colors depending on what the experience has been. These patterns were connected to my lower chakras.

Eckhart Tolle talks about the pain body. When I am working with people, I see their frozen emotions - their pain, hurt, and trauma in the lower chakras of their bodies. It expands and vibrates through their whole body. If these frozen emotions are not healed, they sometimes create sickness and disease. As I was watching the emotions clearing out of my patterns, I saw the patterns shift out of grey, black, brown and into beautiful rainbow colors.

I then started thinking about experiences I wanted to clear, and Jesus said to stop assisting and just let the memories surface from whatever pattern they belonged with.

My body started tingling in light and freedom. I could feel my cells vibrating in light as they continued to clear out my Soul's karmic agreements from this lifetime and beyond.

The first thing I usually ask when Jesus appears and wants me to walk with him is "Where is Frank?" Many times, I am told he is busy, and will be with us soon.

Jesus explained just as many of us on the Earth are healing

and shifting our consciousness, so are many of the higher spiritual Beings in the Spirit world.

Frank is moving into higher aspects, or dimensions, of himself as a spiritual teacher and Spirit guide. I can definitely feel it and see this as he continues to assist in my private sessions and workshops.

I now have an understanding of this and did not ask for Frank. I was very grateful when he magically appeared and sat next to me. I was again with the two most important men in my life. Of course, Jesus, who I have always called my main man and my beautiful son, Frank.

As I sat there, I felt the love, harmony and Oneness with these men who are definitely my heart and Soul. We are one. There was nothing to say; we just vibrated together as One Love.

The old patterns continued to clear, and I could feel myself starting to float beyond any timeline or memories. As I continued to float, I fell asleep, and when I awoke a few hours later, I could feel my body very light and free. It felt new and freer.

This crystal dimension in which I had been vibrating is a generator for many planets to hold the frequency for the Souls who have incarnated onto the Earth, or whose last lifetime was on another planet. Maybe another planet is actually their planet of origin.

CHAPTER TWENTY-EIGHT

Fun with Family in Hawaii

June 16, 2019

After my integration back into Sedona, I once again started feeling unbearable loss and loneliness. I was thinking to myself that this must be what people feel and experience as they get older in life and don't have family support and love.

I had just come back from Sweden where I have so much love and support. My whole body and systems were vibrating in love, harmony, and so much gratitude.

After a year of such incredible loss and grief, a year of letting go of many belief systems and patterns, I could feel that I had cleared many old layers, or stories, out of my bodies and systems.

When I returned to Sweden in 2019 for my tour, I was plugged back into a higher light and love that I had never experienced. With every workshop and event I would do, I kept moving into higher light aspects of myself, out of my grief and loss and into joy and happiness. I was able to take groups into higher spiritual aspects of themselves. Such an amazing time of awakening. I felt myself crying from so much love - the gift and ability to connect with others on this level of love, gratitude, and compassion. We were definitely connecting with each other on a very high, spiritual level, beyond our stories and into the Oneness and heart of love. We had matched and merged with each other in the Christ/God/Source/Love energy. We were One.

As Frank left the world, he shifted me and our whole family unit out of old patterns and stories and back into what is important in life, which is love. My favorite quote has always been "Whatever the question, love is always the answer." After this year, I knew beyond any doubt that love is all there is.

Because I travel so much with my work, and am constantly with people working through their emotions, coming back to Sedona was always a gift, and the opportunity to be by myself and in my own energy this time felt great for the first week, then I started feeling very disconnected from the level of love that I had been experiencing. I felt very let down and felt the loss that I had felt after Frank left. I had been connecting and vibrating in great love and now I felt myself moving collectively back into the pain, the pain body and the fear of what many on the Earth are going through.

I also knew that I had a choice as to where I wanted to connect my energy. I had planned a trip back to Hawaii to celebrate my sister's birthday and to see my daughter and grandchildren. I also wanted to connect with Frank's daughter - my granddaughter - Danilla. After Frank left, I hadn't called her much or connected to her because I felt such a great loss for her in losing her Daddy. They were so close. He was her foundation. She was definitely a daddy's girl. I felt guilty for not reaching out to her, but I was too heartbroken.

My heart felt heavy, and I felt concerned about returning to Hawaii. This would be my first trip back without my family being there for support.

It ended up being one of my best trips and visits.

I had a couple of days to myself before I started emerging into family. The first day, I drove to places where Frank and my daughters, Tricia and Jennifer, and I had lived. I drove by all of the amazing places where my children and I had spent so much time together.

As I drove through memory lane, I was very surprised because all I felt was love, joy, and laughter at the magical life that we had all shared. Of course I had many memories of Frank, but instead of the pain and loss, I felt the love and gratitude for everything we had shared together. I was very grateful that I had so many years with Frank and that we had been very close and shared the same spiritual consciousness.

I could feel Frank with me. I was also experiencing life through his memories of his life with myself and our family. All I could feel was love, joy, and gratitude.

I drove to Kaimana Beach where we had Frank's celebration of life. In some ways, it seemed so long ago, and at the same time, yesterday. I was remembering that we truly celebrated his life, and I could feel the love and joy that we all experienced together as we celebrated him.

I then drove to the other side of a very big park (Kapialani). It is a huge, beautiful park with many banyan trees. I decided to work on the book there.

I took my shoes off to walk on the Earth as Frank was instructing me to do. I could feel the heartbeat and energy of the Earth. I knew I was experiencing the Earth through Frank. He loved being on the Earth in nature and in the ocean. They were his natural home.

I sat at a table underneath a very big banyan tree. Birds were coming up to me, and I became their songs. As I sat in nature, I felt myself on the Earth and yet also shift through many doorways into the spirit worlds or realms. I felt my heart open into the One Love and consciousness of all of Creation.

I was in the bliss and silence of Oneness that I had experienced so often over the last few months. This is who we are; we are not separate from each other. We are One cell of all that is. Every cell of our bodies carries this divine blueprint of love – of One love – and through the loss and gift of our loved ones leaving, our hearts have the ability to open to the memories of who we really are, which is love. If we allow it, our loved ones can assist us to lift the veils or dimensions so we can experience higher aspects of ourselves multidimensionally.

As I sat there in silence within myself, I was also aware of the music of the birds and the majestic beauty of all that was around me. Every cell of my body vibrated in love. There was no story, no loss, only love. I was home in my physical body.

My love frequency was expanding into the trees, the Earth, the ocean, the sky, the birds and all of nature.

The birds must have been experiencing this love because I had put peanuts on the bench, and they were practically eating out of my hand. What a beautiful day and beginning of my trip.

All I could feel was love and gratitude. This was the beginning of a level of love I would continue to expand through me to clear out all of the old stories.

This is the new lifetime's energy. The frequencies are expanding us into a collective Souls Awakening of Love and Oneness.

The rest of my trip, my vacation, continued to expand into joy and laughter.

My sister, Danilla, and I went to the Big Island, Hawaii, to spend time with my daughter, Jennifer, and her children.

I had decided before I left for this vacation, I was going to have fun with Danilla. I have spent a good amount of time with my other grandchildren but not much with Danilla, not much one on one.

I had booked a time on a boat to swim with the dolphins. That morning, I wasn't feeling well so the whole gang went without me. Unfortunately, the dolphins weren't around that morning, but they had a great time snorkeling anyway.

All of my children and grandchildren love to surf, swim, snorkel, paddle; anything they can do in the ocean.

Frank had taught Danilla to surf and to be comfortable with the ocean when she was very young. He had a pink flowered surfboard made for her, which she had definitely outgrown.

We would start our mornings gathered around the Island in the middle of Jennifer's kitchen. While we were having our morning coffee and tea, we would draw angel cards to receive our daily message.

We did many activities that tourists find so inviting, and yet, as locals are our everyday life. Although I don't live in Hawaii now, I consider myself a local because I had lived there for many years.

I was grateful to be able to spend time with family and to form a bond with Danilla. We all had fun, a great time together.

For all of us, Frank's departure has brought us closer together, lifting the veils and connecting our hearts on a deeper level. None of us know how much time we have together or if we will actually see each other again. Seizing the moment and living fully conscious in the now is all there really is.

After my vacation and my return to Sedona, I felt totally renewed. I no longer felt the loneliness. I was love with my family. My whole body felt fed, and my etheric body's DNA system had matched and merged with my family's systems in love, joy, happiness and gratitude.

My last time in Hawaii, our DNA systems had matched and merged in the horrendous loss, grief, and hopelessness of Frank leaving. The pain was so deep and raw, like an open wound that would scab over momentarily but not heal.

This time together, we all felt Frank with us, but in his laughter and joy and in all the memories of love and great times that we had shared together.

His presence was definitely with us, and he was grateful that we were sharing this time together with Danilla, really local style living.

In my third book *The Creator Heals*, the Creator explains that our etheric DNA system is always, always, always matching and merging with our environment. This matching and merging is threaded through lifetimes of old stories.

When we understand this, we can choose what we want to match and merge with. Also, everything is collective, and whatever we are going through is threaded with everyone else vibrating in the same emotional pattern.

I experienced and learned this in 2007 after being diagnosed with uterine cancer. I felt myself go into a fear of death, feeling like I might die from the cancer.

I knew that I didn't think like that, and yet, I was living the experience of death. The Creator then showed me that I had matched and merged with the collective energy of cancer. I was connected to and vibrating in the fear and death cycle of cancer, of those that were dying and those that had already died from cancer.

When I understood this, I was able to disconnect from the pattern of death. This experience led me into the DNA work and healing that I now assist others through in my workshops.

I do believe that everything we go through, our Soul had signed up for to assist us to grow, ascend into unconditional love for ourselves and the world. There are many experiences that I have gone through, that had I remembered I was signing up for, I probably would not have done it. My beautiful son leaving the Earth is one of them. I also believe that there is a light through the darkness, and many times the loss or lesson leads us down a path to assist others that may be going through a similar experience.

When Frank first left, I could not imagine how I would get through it, and now I am sharing my journey to assist others in whatever way that may help.

I have also experienced much of what a person goes through when they leave this world and have had the gift to be able to travel through many dimensions on the other side.

My son, Frank, is one of my angel Spirit guides and teachers. He is also assisting, helping others, as a Spirit guide, teacher and is my assistant in my workshops. He brings great love, laughter, and joy to many.

There is no death; a Soul does not die. The Soul shifts dimensions, changes addresses, and goes home into the Spirit world, into the arms of love.

After a healing reunion and integration, the Souls may stay in Spirit to assist as a guide or teacher or they may wait to begin their next assignment on the Earth or in other dimensions.

CHAPTER TWENTY-NINE

Our Soul's Journey
Coming Down to the Earth

August 10, 2019

I woke up this morning early, 5:00 a.m., and could not sleep. I tried to go back to sleep, but Spirit had a different agenda. I made my connection to Spirit as I do every morning, and my two favorite men showed up and wanted me to walk with them.

I was walking with Jesus and Frank through dimensions that looked kind of gray. The more we walked, I realized I was walking through a very large, crystal passageway. This was a different energy, or color of crystal, than I had ever experienced before. As we continued through this very wide passageway, we came to a road, an area that had many paths and passageways. Some of the roads or paths crossed bridges and then continued through this dimension.

We stopped, and when I looked around, I was surprised at how vast this area was with so many roads that looked like they led to nowhere. As we stood there, Jesus explained that these roads led to the different dimensions from where people were choosing to reincarnate.

When I am working with people, giving them a session, I always experience what I call a waiting dimension. This is a dimension where people are waiting for their exact number to be called to return to the Earth. Their exact number is their whole astrological makeup of their Soul's agreement of what they are choosing to learn, understand, or complete in this new lifetime on Earth.

I always find it interesting when I see what Souls are doing as they are waiting. Many times, I will see a Soul dancing, listening to or playing music. Other times I will see the person taking notes because when they get down here, they want to remember everything they have agreed to experience and heal.

I may see the person I am working with taking notes and other people may be laughing and joking about what they have agreed to go through. Others are so into music that they tune everyone else out. This person is usually nervous about their upcoming journey to the Earth.

In this waiting dimension, if I see that my client really loves music, I will ask if they love music. They will always answer yes that music is their life, or I may see that music feeds their Soul. It is the same with notetaking; the person will share that they always take notes because they don't want to forget anything. If I see them joking around in this waiting dimension, I will ask if they have a good sense of humor, and they will share that humor is what gets them through life.

What I have experienced is that Souls have a personality that follows them through every lifetime.

The problem is that they may choose to be born into a lifetime where music is against their religion or not allowed for some reason. When this happens, the Soul's spontaneous energy, or frequency, is frozen. Many times, they feel numb inside, like they can't breathe or like they are going to explode.

As I am writing this, I am being shown how the Soul gets to their waiting dimension. I am thinking to myself: "Of course! This makes sense. Frank's higher spiritual work is to assist the Souls that are now incarnating to the Earth."

Jesus is showing me that every Soul has its own tone, or song, and color frequency. Souls also have a Soul group, which means they come from the same Master Soul.

The way that it has been explained to me is like a mother giving birth and then the child she births gives birth and the birthing process continues ending up with many children with the same lineage, or DNA systems.

This is how Soul groups are formed. Of course, we can follow the Soul group further back, and we will expand into One Soul, or Cell, of Creator, which is God/Source/the I AM/Allah or whatever your chosen belief or preference as to what is called the Supreme Being. This is the Oneness that so many on the Earth are experiencing and remembering. We are coming home into the One Soul multidimensionally.

All Soul groups have their own color and frequency, and when they come together, they create a symphony of love. The Souls from any group may live many different places in the world. They may be of many different nationalities and religions. All souls actually hold the frequency of the color and sound for each other in their group. This is so they can move through their karmic agreements on Earth and many times on different planets.

I hear people say they feel so alone down here. They are longing to be home in like energy, like consciousness. They feel totally cut off, no connection. This is because they aren't vibrating in their Soul group's frequency. Their own tone has nowhere to connect; there is no place to plug their system in to recharge into their symphony, or song, into their higher frequency that lights them up. They feel as though they have been plopped down here on the wrong planet or in the wrong family unit.

Jesus is showing me that the different roads that I am seeing lead to the many dimensions from which a Soul chooses to incarnate.

If a Soul is incarnating into a family whose religion is Jewish, it will move into the dimension of that frequency. The same goes for Christian, Muslim, or any other religion. At this time, he is showing me religion because that energy is very prevalent on the Earth at this time regarding religious conflicts and wars.

What I find interesting is that many of the religions from the eastern countries that are at war with each other actually carry the same energy frequency.

They are together in the same dimension as they are waiting for their number to be called. And many are actually friends; they like and love each other. It is when they come to the earth that they move into their chosen role or into the karmic lesson that needs to be experienced to move through and healed.

These Souls may even be laughing and joking with each other before they come down here. Remember, I love you ... it's not personal. They have been together before and are completing some lessons with each other.

There may be Souls coming down as atheists, others that will be against God, and they are all in the same waiting dimension as the Christians because they are of the same Soul group and may have the same lessons and intentions of healing in this lifetime. They are holding the energy for one another to get through their Soul's earthly journey.

The dimensions from which we incarnate all carry frequencies and color. Every color has a sound and every sound has a color.

As the Souls are in the waiting dimension, their colors and sounds harmonize with each other. There may be many different aspects of Soul groups in the same dimension. Their experience is like a crystal in a window. When the sun hits its prisms of color, rainbows of color fill the entire room. What we may not understand is that as the crystals are emanating all of their beautiful colors, they are also sending beautiful waves of music through the air, into the Earth's atmosphere. This creates a safe passageway of like energy through which the Soul reincarnates.

The reason Souls gather together in these waiting dimensions is because the Earth's frequencies are lower vibrations than what the Soul experiences when it is at home in their highest light.

If they were to reincarnate from this higher light, they would not match the energy of the parents and systems from which they are choosing to incarnate.

Their frequencies would be too high, and the Soul would not be able to stay in their mother's womb. They would have an electrical blowout, miscarry, or even be born with disabilities. This would also create havoc in their mother's system. It is after the Soul is born that their energy can shift again into their higher frequency. As their energy becomes lighter, it can also be a challenge for the mother, father, and loved ones. The amazing Souls that are coming to the Earth now are very conscious, and their energy definitely activates everyone around them.

The Soul is not totally in the body until it is born. This is how a very high vibrational Soul is able to live in a mother's womb that carries a lot of trauma and fear.

This Soul is still very much in the Spirit world until it moves out of the womb and into the earthly dimension. It can once again expand its light with Spirit.

As our consciousness has shifted, many of these gifted children are being born into family units that have an understanding of this and actually welcome their amazing crystal rainbow child or children. They honor the wisdom that the child is bringing to them and the world.

This light energy and consciousness actually wakes families up and shifts them into a stronger connection to Source/God. They wake up spiritually. For others, the light frequency may activate all of their old hurts and patterns. They may project all of their unhealed emotions, hurt, fear, anger, etc., back onto the light child. The person does not understand why they have a difficult time being with the light child.

The person and the child's energies don't match, like putting a square into a round hole. This is very hurtful and challenging for the child. They start feeling like there is something wrong with them; they don't fit. They don't belong; no one understands, and the child ends up having self-worth issues, not being important or valuable.

As this light child gets older, he may start using drugs, alcohol, food, sex, addictions to cover the pain.

I have worked with and counseled many addicts, and they are always very sensitive and incredible Beings of light.

The Souls that choose the journey of being the light that is not understood usually feel like they are the black sheep of the family. They are actually the light that has agreed to take the whole family through healing processes. These healings are usually not easy. Addiction is a family disease and moves families into forgiveness and eventually letting go. Sometimes the letting go is actually through the loss and death of a child from the addiction. Although heartbreaking, the loss can open the hearts of all involved, opening their hearts to love and what is important in life.

It is important to remember that you chose this lifetime or consciousness on the Earth, and you are in a lifetime of completion. Nothing you go through is new. Every experience has a frame of reference someplace else, meaning from a past life experience.

In a past life, maybe the addict had a child or loved one who was addicted, and they were cruel to the person because they didn't understand addiction. This lifetime for them is to experience the other side of the coin: the experience of the addiction.

People who go through NDEs have the reverse happen for them. As soon as they leave the Earth and go through their tunnel of light (or however their departure happens), they instantly feel an ever presence of love and forgiveness. All of their earthly struggles and challenges instantly disappear. They are home.

Many of them don't want to come back, and those that do usually have a totally different understanding and perception in life, of what is important. Many times, they shift into a larger purpose on Earth and want to serve humanity. They want to educate people about life after life, or death, with the intention to assist people to heal. This service is about love and co-creating Heaven on Earth.

As Jesus and Frank are showing me this, I certainly have an understanding of why we would have waiting dimensions that would slowly lower our vibration to become compatible to live on the Earth's third dimensional frequency.

Our physical bodies would not be able to hold this amount of light and consciousness. Our bodies are carrying many lifetimes of fear, grief, guilt, shame, hopelessness and many more emotions of pain. Our higher light would blow our systems out. We would not know who we are.

We come down here with amnesia, meaning we don't usually remember our agreements, contracts or past lives. We bring people and places into our lives that mirror, activate and awaken many old memories that are stored in our bodies, mentally, emotionally and physically. From the emotional activations of the old patterns, we start slowly unraveling and healing from many old, karmic lifetimes. As we heal our wounds, we have the opportunity to merge back into our light bodies, our spiritual bodies, without leaving our physical bodies.

Before we move into the waiting dimensions that match our chosen earthly journey's energy, we sit in front of a karmic board and decide what our new lifetime's intention and journey involves.

All memories, emotions, karmic contracts and patterns come up at once for you to map out and choose your Soul's next agreed upon assignment. You see and experience your soul's whole journey from the beginning of existence to becoming an individual personality (Soul). Before you become an individual Soul, you were

One collective Soul. From the collective Oneness, you were birthed into an individual Soul or personality and from there began your journey of growth.

As you sit in front of the karmic board, you have a map of all that your Soul has learned and accomplished. You see every lifetime's journey: who you were with, what role you played: male/female, ancestry background, where you lived, your religion – all is shown to you as your Soul's pattern.

You also see what else your Soul needs to learn, where you made mistakes and didn't get the lesson. There is no judgement from anyone and no self-judgement.

This would be like looking at a map and seeing all of the countries that you have visited and experienced – their cultures, religions, etc. As you look at this map, you can see what other country's cultures, religions, ethnic groups, identities and emotions you haven't experienced.

With your spiritual team, you design the new lifetime in which you choose to incarnate. You choose the lessons you need to learn and who you need to learn them with. You can see every person you have been with and all of the different roles that you have played with each other. Maybe in this new lifetime, you will change genders and learn the other side of the lesson through experience.

Perhaps you were prejudiced and now you will choose a lifetime that you are prejudiced against. You choose to experience again what you could not heal or clear in other lifetimes.

Perhaps you lost a child and loved one and were not able to move through the loss. When your loved one died, you basically emotionally died, too. You may choose to go through a similar experience for the outcome to be different. From your loss and grief, you may go forward and assist others to get through their loss.

When our Soul was created, we knew everything but didn't

know how we knew. To learn how we knew, we agreed to separate from the One Soul and become an individual personality. We chose to understand our knowledge by playing every role and having every experience imaginable. From our life's experiences, we have the opportunity to move beyond judgements and into knowing there is only love.

We then live from my favorite quote: "Whatever the question, love is always the answer."

Collectively our Souls have shifted through and conquered many lessons. We are the wings of each other as we move back home into the Oneness, into the One Soul from which we were first created.

After we decide our Soul's chosen journey that we will descend into, we move into a period of what we on Earth call meditation. Through our meditative self and our high self's energy, we merge with our higher spiritual Soul group. We form our whole spiritual support system, our spirit guides, and Masters and teachers who will be guiding and protecting us on our new chosen journey.

When we have mapped out our life and decided every player (person) who will be on our Earth's journey, we connect our energies with theirs and decide exactly what and where we will meet. Our etheric and physical DNA systems have reconnected so that when we come back into the body (our earthly form), we have already downloaded every memory, every lifetime, and every emotion that our Soul has ever experienced. From there we move into the waiting dimensions that are compatible with our new lifetime energetically.

When our exact astrological number is called, when our father's sperm hits our mother's egg, we become an explosion of light moving into a physical form. As soon as we are conceived, we instantly download both of our parents' and ancestors' patterns and karmic agreements into us and we also download all of our karmic patterns, agreements, and emotional contracts into them. In that instant, we become one agreement.

For years, the Creator has shared that we are coming into, ascending into, a new lifetime without physically leaving the body. As was explained earlier, this is happening now. Many incredible children, Souls, are coming to Earth being born fully conscious and are remembering who they are, who God is, and what it's like in the Spirit world. They are actually opening portals of light that are shifting the whole world into higher frequencies.

These high energies are activating the shadow ego part of us to be healed individually and collectively.

Everything is being exposed. It is not an easy time to be on the Earth, and yet it is such a gift. So many of us are shifting dimensions, waking up spiritually many times by going through a "Dark Night of the Soul." Through this awakening, we realize what is important in our life: Love.

As challenging as it may be to be on Earth right now, Souls are still lined up and excited to have the opportunity to come to the Earth.

In my earlier books, the Creator talks about this lifetime being the one of completion for many of us. We have the opportunity to clear and heal many ancestral patterns for ourselves and generations forwards and backwards.

The consciousness that has awakened on the Earth is amazing. So many people are waking up, remembering and downloading incredible information and knowledge.

People are doing great spiritual work and experiencing spontaneous healings.

Years ago, when I started my spiritual path, not much was written spiritually, and now you can find books or Google the internet on any subject imaginable and some that you could not imagine. The history channel is bringing much of our ancient history to light. Years ago, aliens and life on other planets were frightening and foreign to people, and now much of this information is mainstream.

With DNA testing, epigenetics, we are finding out that our species are so much more than we could ever have imagined.

Many people are having spontaneous awakenings, and many are having near death experiences (NDEs) and bringing information back from the Spirit worlds. We are definitely ascending multidimensionally.

I believe it is important to focus on the light and good in the world, and there is so much good. Unfortunately, not enough of the good is being shown and shared with us.

CHAPTER THIRTY

Waking Up in Love, Light, Gratitude and Grace

August 2019

Yesterday, after giving a beautiful woman a past-life, Soul retrieval, healing session, I experienced another level, an explosion of love and gratitude that I had never experienced before.

Frank leaving this world threw me a curve ball, a loss that was unimaginable, and now 15 months later, I am feeling a love that can only be compared to the love in the Spirit world - when we leave our bodies and go home.

The love and gratitude I experienced yesterday definitely shifted me into a higher dimension. All I could feel was love: love for myself and love for everyone's journey down here. Love for the clouds, love for the trees, for the beauty of this world. I felt so much love and compassion for what everyone on Earth goes through. My heart was very open in love. I cried but not from pain; the tears were from love. I felt so much love, gratitude and acceptance of everyone and everything that I didn't quite know what to do with myself. I also felt concern that it might go away. I did not want to lose this experience.

When I woke up this morning, my expanded experience was still here. As I looked around my room, I felt love for all of my plants, for my home, for the safety of having a home. I could feel how very fortunate I am.

When I went into the kitchen to make tea, I felt love and gratitude for having a teapot, for my blender, for my pots and pans, for my dishes, my silverware. I was experiencing how fortunate I am to have so much where some people in our world have nothing. I looked out on my porch and felt the gratitude that I have a nice porch where I can eat with nature all around me. I can enjoy the bird's music.

As I stood there, with every breath I took, I could feel more love expand me beyond my earthly possessions and into the higher picture, knowing of God, the Source. Once again, the love and gratitude were beyond anything I could imagine, and it just kept expanding, expanding, expanding. I was overwhelmed with gratitude and did not want to lose this experience.

As I stood there, I also realized that this is the way Frank felt before he left this world. He was love and always joyful and happy. He savored life and everything he did and talked about was exciting for him.

After he left, his best friend, Joe, told me that if Frank was drinking a cup of tea, he would always express how great it was and that everything he did was the greatest for him as if he was experiencing it for the first time.

I did not really understand because I had never experienced this level of Oneness with God, all life force, on this level. I have certainly experienced God and love. I work in the spiritual dimensions and bring loved ones through for people from the other side or higher dimensions and have gone through an NDE, but this was beyond all of that. This was truly in the heart and Soul of God's love.

When Frank left this world, he was already there. He had already expanded into this amazing love. In this love, all is gratitude. There is nothing that needs to be forgiven. There in only love.

Jesus and Frank have been with me all morning, and Frank has been pretty insistent that I sit down and work on writing this book.

Never in my consciousness or in my life could I ever imagine that Frank leaving could ever have any kind of gift for me. I have always had an understanding that no one ever dies and that they are with us from the other side, and yet not having them in the physical body is such a tremendous loss.

Even though Frank has been with me from the beginning of his departure, I really missed him, and I still miss him here on Earth with me.

I now feel at one with him where there is no separation. When he shifted into higher dimensions, he shifted our whole family unit.

What a gift he gave to all of us. Thank you, my beautiful son, Frank. Thank you for the honor of being your mother. Thank you for choosing me to be your mother. In love and gratitude, I am excited about the many years we will continue to work together. You are the greatest, most conscious assistant that I have ever had, of course with the exception of Jesus.

CHAPTER THIRTY-ONE

Flower of Life / Spiritual Awakening

September 2019

After I woke up this morning, I lay in bed making my connection to Spirit, and I saw and felt Jesus' energy in my 3rd eye. My 3rd eye started opening up, and it became pyramids of crystals. As the pyramids kept expanding into more and more doorways of light, my 3rd eye became the flower of life. The flower of life was all crystals, and each circle of life expanded throughout all of Creation.

As the crystal circles continued to expand, they became the stars, planets, all of Creation, becoming circle within circle, within circle and merging into the Oneness, the One cell of Creation, from which we first began.

Then Jesus asked me to walk with him. He took me into the tunnel of light that so many people speak of as they leave their earthly bodies back home into the Spirit world.

He wanted me to stay in this light with him so I could feel what happens to a person's energy as they shift worlds.

He was showing me through experience how all of the karmic contracts with people start dissolving. When we leave our physical bodies, we no longer carry the emotional DNA patterns of the karmic, or agreed upon lessons, that we needed to learn, understand or complete while on the Earth.

Of course, the Soul still carries the memories but without the physical body of form. We move back into our true state of being, which is love.

When we are first conceived by our parents to come down to

the Earth, every agreement of every experience your Soul has agreed to go through is downloaded into every person who your Soul will be having contact with or meeting.

The contracts with the people you will meet throughout your whole lifetime are already in place; they are already downloaded into their systems. You are already connected to them energetically. This download is like an emotional map that your Soul follows throughout your whole life until the day you take your last earthly breath.

The download of these agreements with the people are like the flower of life. The circle within circles are all of the lifetimes and emotional patterns that you have lived through with each person. In this lifetime now, the agreement is to complete in love.

This does not always mean that the person will still be a part of your life on the Earth. The agreement is for you to complete in love, forgiveness, and eventually gratitude of the gift that you have received from the relationship. Maybe what you are going through with the person does not feel like a gift in the moment of the experience, but as you complete with the person, the gift of freedom will be within yourself.

Many times, the gift is taking your power back from an abusive, toxic experience or environment. From this, you move into a sense of self-love, self-worth, and empowerment. From this gift, you start breaking the pattern for future and past generations.

The circles are what the Creator speaks of in my other books: This is the lifetime of completion, of coming full circle, not just one circle but many circles, with everyone who has agreed to be in your life's amazing journey.

Now, as I am standing in the light tunnel, or doorways, beyond our earthly journey, I am experiencing the opposite of the earthly agreements.

Now that the physical body is gone, I am experiencing ascending into the circles of completion, where there is only light and love. This is our rebirth into our higher selves and into our light bodies.

When we come to the Earth, we download our Soul's journey, when we leave the earthly body, so do the emotions of our earthly agreements and contracts. There is a sense of completion, like a job well done.

Jesus wants me to continue to stand in the light tunnel so I can experience how the transmutation through dimensions happens. I am experiencing this slowly, but when a person leaves their body, it happens almost instantly because there is no time, no past, present, or future. All experience is in the now.

On the Earth, as we collectively are shifting through the circles of ascension portals, we are moving into the light of our experience. This feels like our light has a dimmer switch, and with each karmic completion, our light is continuing to be turned up.

Because of this enlightenment shift, people are collectively moving into the death of their earthly agreements, into the death of the shadow, of the ego, and into the rebirth of forgiveness and gratitude. They move into truly experiencing themselves as One Being of light and love.

Because our light and love has heightened and we are still unthreading from our earthly contracts, our collective light has also activated our own shadow and the collective shadow of fear.

The gift is that all fear is coming to the multidimensional surface for us to know what needs to be healed individually and collectively.

We are the Ones who have agreed to do this job, and we are doing it, shifting our world from fear to love.

As you look at our world, this may not seem true, but look how many millions of people have awakened spiritually, how many people are talking about love, forgiveness, and gratitude. This is the Ascension.

As I am standing in this tunnel of light, Jesus is bringing my whole family unit, my parents, loved ones, and of course, my son, Frank, and all I can feel is love and gratitude. This does not feel like the overwhelming experience of love that I have awakened and shifted through multidimensionally since Frank's departure. This is more a feeling of love and gratitude as a sense of our job was well done – a great completion.

As I am standing there together with my whole family unit, I experience the many different roles and lifetimes that we have all gone through together and have completed in love. I can feel our heart become One heart as we merge together beyond our personalities, beyond our stories, beyond time, and beyond form.

We have moved through the tunnel of light and into our rebirth, expanding multidimensionally, into Love and Oneness.

Jesus is showing me that we are collectively in the tunnel of light. We are going through the same experience of death that we shift through when we physically leave our bodies. We are going through a death of old consciousness. We are ascending beyond our earthly, karmic agreements and contracts. We are in our Soul's rebirth and are shifting into a new lifetime on the Earth; a new lifetime of love, forgiveness and gratitude; a new lifetime of co-creating Heaven on Earth. We are in our own tunnel of light of death (death of karmic agreements, contracts, patterns and into the rebirth of living from our higher selves' consciousness now).

We don't have to wait until we physically die to remember who we are. We are awakening multidimensionally and living from our light body's consciousness. This awakening is actually in our DNA. Through the Earth's ascension, many codes of higher consciousness are being activated in all of us individually and collectively. We are the Ones we have waited for.

CHAPTER THIRTY-TWO

Experiencing Life and Laughter Again

September 2019

It has been a while since I have traveled with my spiritual team into the higher spiritual realms. I was very busy before I left on my Swedish spiritual tour.

I had also met a man with whom I had a short relationship. A girlfriend had invited me out one evening to listen to music. I was very nervous because I had not been out around people socially since Frank's death.

I was sitting with another person, who I knew, while waiting for my friend. I looked over and saw a man leaning against a wall. As we looked at each other, there was an instant connection.

Although our relationship was short-lived, I am very grateful that he came into my life. He was like a life raft. He extended his hand to me and pulled me out of the grief, loss, and "Dark Night of the Soul" in which I had been drowning.

When Frank left, I felt like Humpty Dumpty that fell off the wall. My heart was shattered into pieces, and I didn't know if I would be able to put it back together again. I didn't think that I would want another relationship with a man, that I could love again. This man extended his hand and brought me into his heart and Soul, and I experienced the safety of love again. We had fun and I found myself laughing and wanting to exercise, to feel good about my body again. My life force and will to live, my will to love, had returned.

Our romantic relationship was short-lived, but our spiritual, heart connection and friendship is very strong. I am very grateful that he agreed to come into my life to lift me out of grief ... and to give me the will to go forward. I needed to laugh and experience life and humor again.

During this time, my attention was not on writing this book.

At this time, my mother also came through and communicated with me again from the other side. Her face appeared to me. In her very know-it-all voice, she expressed that she was happy that I was feeling better and also said, "Michelle, you must get this book done."

I knew that Spirit was also pushing me to journal my experiences and to complete this book. They had shared with me that so many people are leaving the Earth now and that their loved ones left behind need to know that their departure from the Earth was by agreement. They need to know that their loved ones are safe and what it is like for them when they return to the Spiritual realms, world, or Heaven.

Spirit wants to share the Spiritual realms with those of us who are still on the Earth.

I am also working on preparing my new program for my short return to Sweden, I was writing the text for my evening lecture and healing that I would be presenting to a group, and the information came through me from my spiritual team that I would be teaching a 21-day healing download for the group. I was surprised and at the same time I knew that Jesus and my spiritual team always bring new information through me to assist people to grow and heal.

CHAPTER THIRTY-THREE

First evening in Stockholm

October 25, 2019

My first presentation of the 21-day download and activation was absolutely incredible and very easy for people to learn.

The evening began with my spiritual team clearing people's bodies mentally, emotionally and physically of old patterns and belief systems. I felt like Spirit had stepped into the room and lifted the veils between our 3rd dimensional world and the realms of the Spirit world.

One woman shared that she could feel Spirit working on her during the process. She felt like she had gone through psychic surgery.

Of course, Frank was there and put his hand into people's thymus (new chakra for our new lifetime on Earth for our new world). Some people refer to the thymus as the high heart. Frank wrapped his hand around the old, emotional energies and stories that were stuck in people's bodies and started pulling the stuck energies, stories, of sickness and disease out of their organs, tissues, cells, and their etheric and physical DNA systems.

While teaching and sharing the 21-day process, I could see people's bodies immediately shift and clear depression, self-worth issues, fear and many other old emotions. The group's auric fields became light and full of crystal-like colors. As the old patterns cleared, people's hearts started opening and the room became one of joy, happiness and light. We all experienced the incredible shift.

Since the first evening, I have taught the 21-day process many times to groups and to my family and friends. In Sedona, AZ where I live, we are having weekly groups where we go through the process together. Doing the healing process alone is very powerful but even more powerful as a group (two or more gathered in my name from Jesus).

When I have grief, loneliness, or my feelings of the loss of Frank surface, I will go into the process and the emotions dissipate and clear pretty quickly. Every time I do the process, I feel my heart opening up into more love and gratitude.

Because this process is so powerful and easy to do, I want to share it with all of you. The testimonials that I have received from people are incredible. After clearing many old emotions, doors are opening for people that they could only hope for but never really imagined.

21-DAY HEALING DOWNLOAD AND ACTIVATION

Make a list of what you want to release and heal and do this technique for 21 days. I have experienced that you can actually release many patterns, belief systems, hurts, and heartaches at the same time.

An example: Mother/Father/God/Creator, I now set the intention and command that every cell of my body, that all consciousness, unconsciousness and subconsciousness of my Being now awaken, know and remember that I am safe to release and clear old patterns, agreements, belief systems, programming of fear, emptiness, loneliness, feelings of worthlessness, depression, hopelessness, grief, loss, confusion, fear of love, betrayal in love, jealousy, envy and anything else that you want to include.

Then give thanks that it is done. Do this every day, and you will be amazed at how much clears from your bodies and systems. You will start feeling lighter, free, happier, and more joyful. You are going through and clearing many layers of old programming. It's like peeling an onion.

After you go through the healing release, you will ask to receive the 21-day download and activation.

Don't worry or be concerned about what is being downloaded into you. Spirit knows what your needs are, and the download is a system upgrade. If you aren't comfortable using my words for God or Creation, use what feels comfortable for you.

TECHNIQUE

21-day cycle — karmic release and light body activations: Go up through the pineal gland in the top of your head. (Your pineal gland is in the middle of the brain and is actually your DNA connection to the heart of Mother/ Father/ God/Creator/Source/I AM.)

Just imagine a cord going up through your body out the top of your head and into the center of God, or whatever your experience or reference of God is, to the heart of Mother/Father/Creator.

SAY: *I now set the intention and command that every cell of my body, that all consciousness, unconsciousness and subconsciousness of my Being now awakens, knows and remembers that I am safe to release and clear (whatever it is you want to let go of) from all of my bodies and systems. Thank You. It is done. It is done. It is done!*

(Remember that the reason we give thanks that it is done is because in the higher dimensions it is.)

Wait a few minutes to allow the release to clear from your bodies. Even if you cannot feel it at first, it is happening.

NEXT, SAY: *Mother/Father/God/Creator, I am now ready to receive my 21-day download and activation. Thank you. It is done. It is done. It is done!*

Wait to allow your download to fill your bodies and systems with the upgrade.

CHAPTER THIRTY-FOUR

Healing and Clearing Past Programming

October 31, 2019

I have been back in Sweden for a week beginning my six-week tour.

As I lay on my bed this morning with the intention to meditate, I started chanting "Ma Ma Ma," Mother Mary's chant, and I felt and experienced my heart opening through many layers of light. It felt like white silk curtains flowing open.

I kept traveling through many layers of light and found myself standing with Jesus in the center of a crystal light portal. Everywhere I looked, I saw layer upon layer of crystal realms of light. There was no end to the layers of light. They kept unfolding through what seemed like infinity.

Jesus then reached out and took my hand into his. As he held my hand, different segments of my life started surfacing and like clouds would puff away. I felt no emotions connected to the stories.

I had memories that I had not remembered surface and blow away. As I watched, I saw the different segments of my life appear. My childhood was one segment, and all of the memories would appear and clear away almost as soon as they appeared.

Then my first marriage, the birth of my children and all of the memories of that time of my life appeared and blew away.

I was watching a movie, or a series of my life, divided in segments. As each cycle, or segment, of my life would appear and blow away, another segment would appear and clear.

When I was complete with my life's clearing, I walked down

a crystal walkway with Jesus and I saw Frank standing in front of the outdoor pavilion where he was once again talking to the Souls that were getting ready to reincarnate, or rebirth, to our Earth's world.

This time I walked over to him and felt very comfortable with him in this dimension. Somehow, I knew that a higher part of me, or higher aspect of myself, is working there with him just as he is assisting me here on Earth in my workshops and private sessions.

The contrast between us has somehow dissolved, and I feel more at one with him – no separation. In some ways, I felt a little better with the contrasts. I could see him and feel him separate from me in his own body as my son Frank.

We still have our own personalities but now vibrate together beyond our earthly bodies and the life we had shared together on Earth.

Our higher selves, higher aspects of ourselves in the Spirit world, have merged together as One Heart and One Being of light to be of service to assist our world to heal, to live beyond duality and separation. Our agreement is to assist people, Souls, to awaken, to remember that they are Spirit in a physical body and that there is no death. When we leave this world, we just change addresses; we shift, drop our physical bodies, and awaken into our light bodies.

As I write this, I know that some of what is being said is repetitious, but as we read or hear things a few times, the information registers with us. We understand why we are going through something or why an experience is happening.

We have lived many lifetimes, and this is the lifetime we have agreed to come full circle, meaning this is the lifetime to release and clear all karmic agreements and contracts, to move out of fear and back into love.

Because we have lived many lifetimes, we have old patterns, agreements, contracts and emotions that need to be cleared and healed. All emotional experiences are surfacing in this lifetime for us to heal and clear.

Every experience that you have gone through in this lifetime has a frame of reference in the past, in another lifetime. As you heal the emotions from the other lifetimes, the patterns that have carried over into this lifetime also heal and disappear.

Healing and clearing your bodies and systems from past programming and belief systems is like peeling an onion. As each layer is removed, you feel freer and happier. Many times, sickness and disease disappear. Your relationships become easier. You are no longer communicating from your patterns with one another. You start communicating from your heart of love.

Many times, the old patterns are connected to the ego. Patterns actually become their own entity, or person, and they know where your weaknesses are and how and when to step in and control you.

These patterns may have been handed down to you and you are playing out your parents' and ancestors' patterns of fear, insecurity, old self-worth issues, and lack, etc. You become an extension of your ancestral patterns.

When you understand that you are playing out old programming, you have the opportunity to heal and shift the patterns for yourself and generations forwards and backwards. As you heal and clear the programming you will not pass it on to your children and future generations.

I am explaining this because throughout the book, Jesus and the Masters continue to clear old programmings out of my bodies and systems. It looks like it is the same experience and yet each time a clearing or healing takes place, another layer of the patterns or agreements shift and I become lighter and freer until I move into the core or center of my own self-love and acceptance.

This was my experience while Jesus was holding my hand. I saw segments of my life appear and clear, like clouds blowing away in the wind, but felt no emotions connected to the experience.

As you look at your life, you may feel or experience that you have lived many lifetimes in this lifetime.

When I look back at my younger years in this lifetime, I absolutely am not the same person. These were the karmic completions and segments of my life that Jesus was taking me through or showing me. They had released and cleared. I was only observing the patterns but had no emotional attachment.

CHAPTER THIRTY-FIVE

Love is All There Is!

November 2 - 3, 2019

I just finished a workshop up north of Sweden in Ornskoldsvik. Once again it was the highest energy that has ever come through to work with a group.

As I continue to release and clear my old, hurtful, frozen emotions from my subconscious mind and bodies, I have more room inside of me for Spirit to come through.

It was also the easiest workshop that I have ever facilitated. Spirit and I had become one energy flow. I had no idea of what was going to come through as Spirit and I became one flow of love.

At the close of the first day, the group came together in a healing circle and all we could see and experience with one another was love.

None of us had anything to say to each other. The love that permeated through us left us in love and gratitude. We really were One Love vibrating in silence where no words were needed.

I could feel Frank with us, and the song "One Love" by Bob Marley came into my mind. I knew the message was from Frank. I had to smile to myself. He loved Bob Marley.

The next day was even brighter. After the workshop people were asking me to please come back again. When are you coming back? I had to laugh to myself. We all wanted more of this unconditional love.

The love moved us beyond any belief systems, programs, stories or injustices. This is the love that people experience when they leave the Earth into the Spirit world. We immediately move

208   SURFING THROUGH HEAVEN'S DOORWAYS

beyond our earthly emotions into love, forgiveness and gratitude.

Many times, in the past after facilitating a great workshop, I would go back to wherever I was staying and would feel let down and alone. This time was different; all I could feel was love, and the next day I felt very free, light and happy.

As I expressed earlier, never in my life did I think I could ever feel gratitude or that there was any gift in Frank leaving this world. When he left, my heart shattered. I was broken open. As I started releasing my pain and grief, I started experiencing that I actually had more room to feel love for others. My heart is very open, and I have love and compassion for other people's lives and journey.

I am able to experience a new expanded level of love that I had no idea even existed. I had always felt love and compassion for others, but now there is no filter. I see and experience the world and all of us here through the heart of Christ's I AM love, through a higher lens of perception.

I am very grateful that my heart and mind are the heart and mind of God and grateful that my son is still very much with me and is my constant assistant in my spiritual work. Thank you, Frank. I love you, honey.

November 6, 2019
21-Day Process / Activation

Every morning I am continuing to ask for my 21-day download. Spirit's instructions were to set an intention as to what we wanted to clear from our conscious, unconsciousness, and subconscious mind and bodies. This morning, I asked to clear any old self-worth issues that may still be hiding and hindering me from moving forward in any way.

As soon as I asked, I could feel Spirit pulling the old programming patterns out of my bodies and systems. It felt electrical, like old cords had been cut and had not been reconnected yet.

I had experienced this before. It felt like strings were unraveling from my bodies. This was the experience that I felt when Frank came to me in the dream and said that I needed to forgive him for leaving.

When he left, my connection, my love and my heart with him had been severed. I felt like live wires were open and my body had no place to reconnect, to ground themselves.

The strings being pulled out of me were old, electrical, frozen emotions. Once again, I was very aware of how these old, fearful patterns run through our bodies and systems. If we don't heal and release these old patterns, they affect us by closing our systems down through sickness and disease.

I have worked on healing myself for many years, and I am always so amazed at how much our bodies hold inside. There really is no past, present or future, and every experience we have ever gone through, from all lifetimes, is still in the cells of our physical bodies.

We bring the experiences from other lifetimes into this one to heal and clear. As soon as we are born, our subconscious mind downloads all memories into our physical bodies.

After this incredible clearing this morning, I asked for my spiritual download and I felt my whole body fill with so much light and love. The frayed edges of the emotions that had been cut and cleared were now reconnected into love.

I could definitely feel a healing had taken place. My body felt light and free. My cells were actually tingling. When I stood up, I felt very light, happy and joyful. As we clear the old memories out of our bodies and systems, we have more room to expand into our true state of consciousness, which is love, joy, gratitude, and freedom.

November 8, 2019
Awakening Self-Love

I woke up again this morning feeling great love and peace. My self-love just kept expanding. I could even hear the voice in my head, the voice in my mind that always sends thoughts to me saying, "Michelle, I love you."

I felt like a dance inside of me. Love, light and joy kept swirling through me, flowing so freely, creating a vortex of love and freedom.

The voice in my mind kept saying, "I love you, Michelle." The voice kept getting stronger, and I became the frequency and voice of self-love. I wrapped my arms around myself, hugged myself and felt incredible love and appreciation for myself, just for being me.

At that moment, I had become the Beingness of the collective consciousness of love. I had never experienced anything like this. Of course, I have experienced love, but never this level of self-love. I was contained in love.

I had a laundry time booked this morning. I am staying with a friend in Stockholm. She lives in a very large apartment complex, and the laundry facilities are six floors down the stairs in the basement.

There are two very big laundry rooms and if you book a time you have the room for three hours. As I took my laundry through the hallways to my laundry room, I was almost singing good morning to everyone I met or saw along the way.

I felt like I was in a musical movie, in one of the old movies where Fred Astaire and others danced. I actually wanted to click my heels together like I have seen in old time movies but thank God my conscious mind knew better than to do that! I probably would have broken a leg or something.

I continued to feel the song and dance inside of me. I felt great love, joy and happiness for me, for Michelle. This experience was not about any love outside of myself; I was contained in self-love.

Had I really reached that state of completion? Love has always been my quest in life. When I was lonely, all I ever wanted was love. As a child, I used to cry to myself, "Love me. Someone please care about me." I was always so alone and afraid.

Many people ask for enlightenment. I always asked God for love. In my emotional and physical body, I am now experiencing love beyond anything I could have imagined, and it is self-love.

I have experienced this love while in the Spiritual realms with Jesus, the Creator and my spiritual team but have never felt myself so full of self-love in this earthly dimension. As I thought of others, all I could feel was love for everyone, and love for their journey and for everything they had signed up to go through in this lifetime.

This intense love and joy lasted all day. When I went to bed that night, I could still hear my own mind and voice expressing love to myself. "I love you, Michelle." With every expression of love, I felt ripples of energy continue to flow through me. I felt like a light bulb of beautiful colors.

Every color has a sound, and as the colors continued to flow through all dimensions of my Being, I felt like a symphony of love expanding through me as my earthly Being and my spiritual Being (my higher self) integrated as One Being.

I fell asleep vibrating in the heart of One Love. I was Heaven on Earth.

CHAPTER THIRTY-SIX

Healing Our Original Split From Source

November 12, 2019

I am up north in Sweden in the town of Umea. I just finished another evening of the 21-day download. It was a very powerful evening with so many people clearing old, fearful, memories and experiences. I am definitely experiencing that the more I clear out old layered programs and patterns within myself, the higher my spiritual vibration is becoming. I am able to bring much higher energies and vibrations through to assist others to heal. As we clear the old out of our bodies, we match and merge with our higher light spiritual team.

Although Jesus has always been with me and taught me my spiritual work, I have never experienced myself in this high level of light and healing energies with him.

I am also experiencing this in my private sessions with others. Before I even put my hands on people, visions of emotions that are holding the person in old, fear patterns surface.

As I take them into prior lifetimes to release the patterns in this lifetime, I am amazed at how deep I am able to go into their bodies. I see many layers clearing that were not reachable before now. I see a deep clearing from their bodies that has been stored in their cells from ancient times.

The old emotion coming out of their cells and bodies looks dusty and moldy.

As I watch this old energy clear, I marvel at what incredible Beings we humans are. We are able to function down here on Earth when we are carrying in our bodies and systems the whole history of our Soul's journey and the history of humanity from this world and beyond.

As a species, we are stronger and more intelligent than we could even imagine.

My clients are also experiencing how deeply and quickly these releases and healings are taking place. I am witnessing them move very quickly out of their emotional stories and into love, forgiveness, compassion, and freedom

Although I am having incredible healing sessions with many people, I woke up yesterday feeling like my body was on fire from pain. I had never experienced fear on this level. I wasn't consciously feeling fear in my mind, but the cells in my body felt like they had been opened up and were on fire from fear.

This was somewhat the way I felt when Frank left only on a different level. With Frank, my cells felt a separation of loss and grief. Now, my cells were separate from my connection with Spirit and were on fire from fear. I actually felt like my cells were alive and burning from the inside out.

This fear was very familiar; it was the fear that I felt much of my life in the morning as I woke up.

Some mornings I would wake up so afraid and alone. Through connection to God and my spiritual team, I was able to get up and function. Sometimes the fear would be so overwhelming and paralyzing that it was hard for me to make a phone call, answer the phone, or even be around anyone.

I had no idea from where this level of fear originated. I knew I had a challenging childhood and life. I had worked on healing my inner children and emotions for many years.

But the amount of fear and pain I was feeling this morning felt almost unbearable. I asked Jesus to help and he magically appeared and asked me to walk with him into the light. As we walked in the higher dimensions of light, I could feel some of the pain start to subside. We walked through a tunnel of light and out onto a beautiful rainbow plateau in the middle of the golden field where I had been taken many times to meet Frank.

As I sat with him, the whole earthly story, my history, woke up within me. I just saw and knew everything at once. This experience was not like a movie or picture unraveling. It was like a history lesson from the beginning of my existence to the end in one flash.

I just knew what he was showing me. He then took me into the experience of our original split from Source from the One Soul, or Cell, from which we were first created. In 2017, The Creator had taken me into this Oneness and healed my MS diagnosis. I was now being shown and reliving the beginning experience of our agreed upon split from the Oneness of Creation, our original split from source.

Jesus was showing me through feeling that because of my high level of spiritual awakening that I was now experiencing, that my own self-love had activated the original split from source. My cells were in shock, and I was afraid and felt very alone.

As I said, this was the fear feeling that I have experienced so much in my life. Everything was making sense to me now.

The Spirit world has always been easy for me to access and has been my healing sanctuary. Jesus was showing me that because I spend much time there in my sleeping state, that when I came back into my body full of my higher light, it would activate within me, duality and my split from the higher light.

Now that I have integrated and am living within my higher light in my physical body, this light once again activated my original split from Source.

Because of this, my body and cells had felt disconnected like there was no place to reconnect, to feel safe.

Jesus asked me to bring the third eye of God/Creation into

me, and I could feel myself calming down as the energy from this higher consciousness was rethreading my cells beyond all of the old stories of separation.

I could also feel the old fear, pain and loneliness start dissolving, dissipating, and my cells were opening up to my birthright and homecoming of love. They were reconnecting to light. They had felt like electrical cords that had been cut but were still emitting electricity and short-circuiting me. Now they were reconnecting to their true source, of God, of love.

I was now feeling very joyful, free and safe with Jesus in this dimension ... another level of love, of homecoming for me, within me.

As I sat there with Jesus, all I could feel was our One love. In this energy, there is no need for words.

This was the same love that I had experienced on the Earth in my last workshop. At the end of the day, there were no words needed. We just looked at each other as we melted into One heart of love.

The love with Jesus was filling and healing my whole body's cells and systems.

Soon, my other main man, Frank, appeared and sat next to me. As we looked into each other's eyes, there was a deep appreciation of love and gratitude that we had been on the Earth together and now we have the gift and privilege of being able to serve God and humanity from our higher consciousness.

Frank, Jesus and I sat there in silence and love.

November 15, 2019

I woke up this morning with my man Jesus asking me to walk with him into higher dimensions. We went through many passageways and dimensions and into a beautiful crystal gazebo where I experienced myself totally free from my original split from Source. I felt and feel a great sense of peace and serenity.

The old fear that had consumed much of my life was totally gone. Once again, Frank came and sat with us. My heart was so alive and yet very peaceful, full of love and gratitude. Never in my life or dreams could I ever have imagined myself sitting in these dimensions with my son and Jesus.

And somehow, I knew our healing journey had just begun. Not the karmic, pain body journey. We had already done that, but my higher spiritual journey with the most important men in my life.

I am humbled, in awe and gratitude.

CHAPTER THIRTY-SEVEN

Frank as My Spiritual Assistant

November 23 – 24, 2019
Two-day Stockholm Workshop

Frank, along with my whole spiritual team, was very present during the whole workshop. He is definitely my assistant. His presence is felt by everyone in the workshop.

As I mentioned before, his work is to assist us to fully awaken our higher spiritual selves into our physical bodies now, co-creating Heaven on Earth.

His new spiritual work is to assist us to ascend into our new lifetime without physically leaving our bodies.

Of course, I am the spokesperson for him, but many also receive his messages directly.

One of the processes Frank took the group through was actually the highest of the weekend. He led them somewhere to retrieve (through Soul retrieval) an aspect of themselves that had been left behind in another lifetime. As they brought the missing piece of their Soul back into themselves now, they felt a sense of wholeness.

People in the group were sharing how powerful it was, that they were feeling a sense of completion within themselves.

Frank also comes through with great humor and joy.

Before every process that the group is taken through, Frank, along with my spiritual team and the group's spiritual team assists to clear frozen emotions and energies out of people's bodies and systems. As I mentioned before, Frank always works with and clears the thymus, the new lifetime chakra. When clearing out the thymus, he will wrap all of the old programming around his hand and pull and clear it out of the liver, gallbladder, stomach, intestines and all of the body's systems. At the end of the process, many times he will place an aqua crystal in the thymus. Aqua/turquoise is the color of the new lifetime into which we are emerging.

I was explaining the 21-day process to the group, and people were asking so many questions. I wanted to move on into the next process because a couple of people in the group needed to leave early to be able to catch a train home.

I guess my tone must have sounded a little impatient because my assistant, Frank, said to me, "Have patience, mom." I started laughing out loud as I shared with the group Frank's message to me.

Unfortunately, when my kids were young, there were many times when I could have been more patient. Frank certainly knew that side of me.

When Frank communicates with me, it is always with great love, joy and compassion.

At that time, he also shared with the woman sitting next to me, (the woman who had brought me the angel wings the prior year, after Frank passed) "Yes. That's my mom!" He was joyful and repeated it to her a couple of times.

In another process, one of the women brought Archangel Gabriel to her, and Frank again was laughing and said, "Oh, now you're bringing on the big boys!"

Because Frank is with me so often, sometimes I forget that he is no longer on the Earth plane with me.

After these great events, I sometimes look at his picture and a great sense of sadness comes over me that he is no longer with us on the Earth, and I cry. I miss receiving his loving phone call and hearing his voice in this dimension. "Hey, mom. I just called to tell you I love you."

The tears don't last very long. I am very aware of how blessed

I am to have him working with me, guiding me and others.

Along with Jesus and my spiritual team, Frank is officially my main Spirit guide.

He has also come through to many others as a Spirit guide. He loves the work he is now doing and is grateful to be able to assist so many on the Earth in their Soul's Awakening.

He is very excited to be able to assist in this great shift, the ascension, and the collective awakening of the consciousness on our planet.

November 27, 2019

The following week, I was facilitating a healing evening for a small group of women. During the process, Frank asked one of the women to walk with him and he took her into the Akashic records. She said to him, "Your mom is guiding us somewhere else, and Frank replied, "Yes, but this is more important."

The previous weekend this woman had already experienced in the workshop the process that I was taking them through. He was not in competition with me; he just knew how important it was for him to assist this woman to clear a karmic program with a man who had been bothering her.

He was coming to her as a guide and let her know that she would feel his presence with her on the right side of her neck, where her neck and shoulder meet. That is exactly the same place his energy connects and communicates with me.

Later that week, I was giving the same woman a private past-life, Soul retrieval session. Afterwards, she said that Frank had been holding her hand while we cleared the past-life trauma from her bodies and systems. He is definitely our protector.

CHAPTER THIRTY-EIGHT

Love, Peace and Gratitude

December 11, 2019

This morning as I lay in bed, I made my connection to my spiritual team as I do every morning. My heart felt so full of love, peace and gratitude.

I am feeling a depth of love and acceptance for myself and others that I did not know existed or could be possible. My many layers of fear of love have dissolved, and all I see and feel is love for people and their Soul's journey. I know being on the Earth is not easy, but it all is certainly worth it.

This morning all of my memories of fear, of loss, and of grief connected to love surfaced. I didn't feel any of the frozen emotions that had gripped me in fear for so many years. I was just watching the memories surfacing as I had done when taken into the review room in the Spiritual realms. I could feel I had cleared the emotions of the stories and now the source of the stories were surfacing, so I could clear the pattern.

This review was putting all of the pieces together like a dot-to-dot puzzle.

On my Swedish tour that I just completed in October 2019, I was taking people into a process of not being safe, and I started coughing uncontrollably. I was also coughing up phlegm from my lungs, from my heart.

I could feel I was releasing the pain of Frank leaving, but I also knew on some level that what was clearing went further back than the loss of Frank.

I was witnessing the death of my 24-year-old cousin, Mary. I was 12 years old and babysitting for her the night she was killed in a car accident. She left behind three very young children.

After her funeral, no one in my family ever talked to me about her death again. I was in grief and pain for many years. I was in India in 2004 and went through a near death experience (NDE), and I found myself floating into a golden field full of many beautiful golden flowers. In the middle of the field sat my cousin Mary. She was beautiful and very full of lifeforce and joy, just as she had been on the Earth.

She talked to me and also asked me to contact her daughter, Maryetta, when I returned to the US, which I did. Maryetta said it was the first time that she knew her mother had loved her. Her mother, Mary, adored her and her two other children.

After meeting Mary on the other side, my heart was able to heal, let go of the painful memory.

Next, I saw a picture of my Aunt Cecile's death. Cecile was absolutely unconditional love.

Mary was the second child that Cecile lost. She had a little girl, Harvetta, die when she was about two years old from pneumonia.

As I look back, I am amazed at how much Cecile was able to continue life and open her heart to the unconditional love that she gave to all of us.

Cecile was the foundation for me and my four siblings. She just loved us, no matter what we did. She saw the positive in most situations. I don't know how I could have gotten through life without my Aunt Cecile.

Maybe the loss of her children broke her heart open to what is important in life, which is love.

The next picture I saw was the loss of my Grandma Amy.

A few years ago, I was facilitating a workshop and spirit asked our inner children to take us someplace. My little girl took me to my Grandma Amy to sit on her lap. I could feel her love for me.

This memory of her love certainly opened my heart to be able to receive love on another level.

I was also able to see and witness my confusion about love. My programming of love had been loss and guilt.

I can remember when I was younger making up my mind that I would never let anyone know that I love them because if I did, they would leave me. I can't remember what age I was, but I certainly remember the agreement I made with myself.

This agreement did not include my children. I always let them know how much I loved them. Many times, we become an extension of our childhood patterns, playing out our childhood again and passing these patterns on to our children.

For many, we choose to learn from the childhood and do the opposite of the pattern, which I did.

Before Frank left this world, he shared with my daughter, Jennifer, that he always knew how much I loved him.

As I lay here this morning watching all of these old stories, patterns, unravel all I can feel is much love and gratitude for my parents, ancestors and their lives. What a gift my life is. I am able to move beyond the stories and into total love and acceptance of my life's journey. I am able to move into the larger picture of what people go through, how they ended up the way they are and how their beginning patterns have co-created their life now.

I am seeing that when I was coughing and spitting up phlegm, that not only was I releasing the loss of Frank, but all of the other losses in my life and also my conflict and confusion connected to love.

I know I was also releasing other lifetimes when the loss of love was too painful to move through.

When we go through big emotional changes in our lives, the emotions actually trigger the subconscious mind to open up and release similar memories of past-life experiences.

When Frank left, my heart broke open and triggered, unbeknownst to me at the time, all other losses of love.

I am very grateful for this blessing and the gift to be able to assist others out of heartbreak, to open their hearts to love.

I am not grateful that Frank left, but I am grateful for the many gifts I have received and am continuing to receive from the loss, and grief. My greatest gift has been the gift of unconditional love for myself and others.

I am now able to look at him and our life together as a blessing for all of the years I had with him and for all of the love we shared on the Earth.

As I lay here, my mother is once again appearing to me. This time her voice is much softer, not her authoritative voice but a voice of love. I could feel her love for me and how proud she was of me and how grateful she was that I had agreed to clear the karmic DNA for our family unit.

She wasn't loving and supportive of me while she was on the Earth, but she sure stepped in at a very crucial time in my Soul's journey. I knew I was leaving the Earth, dying after Frank left, and she also knew it. She kept me here, stayed with me until my Spirit was solid in my body again. She also healed our relationship from the Spirit world from the other side. She wanted and wants what is best for me in the highest. I am very grateful and feel her love and support.

She came to me this morning to let me know that we are complete now. We completed in love.

She was expanding out of our earthly journey and agreement together. She was expanding into higher vibrations of herself just as Frank had done.

I am happy for her; I also feel complete. I know her life on Earth wasn't easy, and I think I was probably the one person on Earth that she needed to complete with, and she did.

SURFING THROUGH HEAVEN'S DOORWAYS

Soar on, Mom. Have a great afterlife. Thank you for agreeing to be my mom and thank you for all of your love and support that you have given me from the other side.

I love you, Mom — my mom, Norma Vivian.

I know it is because of you that I am still alive in my physical body on the Earth now. Had you not stepped in and stopped me from leaving my body, I would not have the opportunity to experience the amazing life that I have awakened into now. I am definitely in a new lifetime on Earth without leaving my physical body. And ... I get to work with my beautiful son. My heart is so full of love and gratitude.

Thank you, Mom.

A Time of Celebration / Freedom

March 8, 2020

This morning, as I was beginning to write the completion of the book, Frank and Jesus dropped into the room with me.

Frank has not been around me for a few days, and I could very much feel his absence, the loss of him.

When I asked where he had been, he shared that he, Jesus and the higher spiritual teams have been celebrating with many Souls that are getting ready to return to the Earth.

These Souls are many of the Masters and teachers that are lowering their vibration to come down to the Earth. These are the Souls that are incarnating fully conscious.

They are lowering their vibration to descend into the Earth's atmosphere. While in their mother's womb, they will have their whole spiritual team around them to hold the higher light frequency.

After they are born, they will be able to turn their vibration up again. They have to lower their vibration while in the womb because their high frequency may not match their mother's emotional bodies. This is to protect their mother's body from short-circuiting and blowing out.

As was explained in the book, Souls incarnating to Earth will come down through different color/sound frequencies of light. This depends on which religion or ethnic group they are choosing to live in.

The frequencies and colors are different, but none are better or worse, lower or higher, than the other; they are just different.

Jesus and Frank are explaining about all of the celebrations, or parties, that they have been assisting and facilitating for the Beings that are getting ready to incarnate.

This is a celebration of a rebirth for the Souls and also for the rebirth of our planet.

In the higher realms, there is much excitement for the shift of consciousness that these Souls are bringing to Earth. A huge multidimensional celebration is happening.

As they are sharing this with me, I feel great light, joy and happiness.

Many of us on the planet are the light holders for the next wave of Ascension. Our spiritual awakening has shifted the consciousness of our planet into a higher light. This has opened portals of light for the Beings/Souls that are coming down to Earth now.

These doorways of light will not close. They are portals that have opened beyond time. Souls coming down are descending through these timelines. Souls that are leaving the Earth are also leaving through these portals.

As we mentioned, many Souls are leaving the Earth now. Their earthly contracts are up. And they are ascending and merging with their higher selves in the Spiritual world.

For those of us who have agreed to stay on the Earth, we also have the opportunity to merge with our higher self in our physical bodies. We don't have to wait until we die to remember who we are.

We are multidimensional Beings, and we are awakening, shifting, into higher aspects of ourselves, into a higher knowing. The Creator talks about us coming into a new lifetime on Earth. We don't have to physically leave our bodies.

This higher shift of consciousness is also termed as Walk-ins. The Walk-in chapter is the last chapter of this book.

What an incredible, multidimensional journey we have signed up for. We are so blessed to have the veils of illusion lift. We get to experience Heaven on Earth within ourselves now.

We have the opportunity to celebrate life and to remember what is important in life: LOVE.

As we stay connected to our higher self as our guiding light, our Soul's earthly journey becomes much easier. We can let go, surrender, and put our seat belts on for an amazing life journey into the heart and love of our Soul's Awakening.

Let's enjoy the ride as we continue to hold the light and love for each other to move into the higher consciousness of our Being. We are the wings for each other.

The one thing I have learned through my "Dark Night of the Soul" journey is that I could not have a gotten through it without all of you.

I thank all of you who have been my wings, who have held me, supported me and even cried with me.

We are here to do this life together.

I love you. I honor you for your agreement to come to the Earth at this time of our incredible Soul's Awakening.

In love and gratitude, Michelle

The other night, I could see Frank in front of me, and he wanted me to dance with him. I danced with him and could feel his support and love for me.

After the dance, we were sitting together, and I noticed that I also was dressed in white. I was surprised, and Frank said to me, "You just got married, Mom."

Hmm, interesting. I don't know if that is the marriage within myself of coming back together in balance, or if I will actually be getting married.

I guess we will have to wait until the next book to know the answer.

From my heart to yours,
Namaste, Michelle

Walk-ins

There are two different kinds of walk-ins. I will explain. For many, walk-ins are higher aspects of a person that agrees to integrate with them. The person's experience of shifting multidimensionally into higher aspects of themselves is happening on the Earth at this time for many.

We as a human species are becoming much more evolved in physical form than has ever happened before on Earth. We have had civilizations that were evolved but ended up in their ego and the civilizations came to an end: such as Lemuria, Atlantis, Egypt, the rise and fall of the Roman Empire, etc. Many times, power becomes greed. It may seem as though the same thing is happening now, which it is, but the outcome gets to be different.

Many of us on the Earth now have lived in these evolved civilizations and carry a memory within us of the rise and fall of the consciousness. Because of this, people on the planet are waking up, speaking up, and remembering that we are really One consciousness, and now we are coming back together in love and gratitude. We are wanting for our neighbor what we desire and want for ourselves.

Many children being born on our planet now are coming through very conscious of life in many forms. Children are coming through knowing who God and Spirit are. They are remembering the Spirit world, and many remember that they have lived other lifetimes. These children are also the future of our world and eventually will step into places of power, into our political arena, and shift us collectively.

This higher, spiritual consciousness is light, love, support, gratitude, honesty, integrity – Oneness.

Many people are waking up spiritually as the veils are being lifted and many are having near death experiences (NDEs). They are bringing to the world the light and information of what life is like in the Spirit worlds.

Many people such as myself are mediums and are able to connect with loved ones on the other side and bring love, support and some kind of closure for those left behind here on Earth.

This is the Ascension that we are all moving through.

We are moving into higher vibrations of ourselves as we collectively are shifting into our higher selves multidimensionally.

Souls are multidimensional. Just as we on Earth use about 10% of our brain, it is the same with our connection to our Oversoul. In the past, we had access to only about 10% of our connection to our Oversoul. Our Oversoul has every memory that our higher selves have ever gone through in any lifetime. It has the memory bank of the gifts we have received, and all that still needs to be completed.

Our Oversouls carry 90% of our higher consciousness that is waiting to be activated, downloaded and remembered!

Our higher self is our guiding light, our higher connection to the Spirit world. Our Oversoul is the collective consciousness of all higher selves, experiences and agreements.

Our higher self guides us, and our Oversoul guides our higher self.

People are now able to connect and communicate with their higher selves as their guiding light.

Our higher self is also multidimensional and can bring us information of our Soul's journey that is absolutely beyond anything that we can perceive or understand in this lifetime.

When a walk-in of our own Soul takes place, it is usually after or in the process of a "Dark Night of the Soul." The experience that we are going through seems like it may be too emotionally painful and difficult to get through.

In our sleeping state, we are in the Spirit world with our higher self, the higher aspect of our Souls, our Oversouls and our whole spiritual team. We then go through the same process as our original birth. We sit with the Akashic record team and our whole spiritual team and decide which higher aspect of our self would be the best match for the personality that now occupies the body.

The higher Soul coming in has the assignment of healing and completing the original Soul's karmic agreements and contracts. When the higher Soul of the person comes in, a drastic and dramatic shift of consciousness usually takes place.

The original personality may feel like it is at the end of being able to handle life on Earth. This person usually has much life experience and hurtful emotions that they have agreed to heal for themselves and their whole family. Their higher intention is to assist others to heal from healing their own karmic journey.

This may be the intention before the Soul came to the Earth, but in the middle of life's painful drama, the Soul may feel like it is too much to handle and becomes suicidal or just wants to leave. They may also end up with a life-threatening disease, heart attack, or in some kind of accident. As they move out of the 'Dark Night of the Soul,' they usually feel like they want to help or assist people who have gone through a similar experience. They want to somehow make a difference in the world. They move out of the I ME and into a larger picture of life and into the I AM.

When a person goes through a life-challenging experience and many times don't know if they are going to survive it, they usually start appreciating life, how short this lifetime is and how important it is to love and forgive.

They move out of the karmic pain body and into a higher perception of life.

When this happens, the higher aspect of the Soul comes in to complete the assignment. As the higher aspect cleans up the painful emotions of the original personality, it usually shifts the whole family unit out of painful emotions and patterns.

Maybe the original personality had been sexually abused and the pattern of abuse was in the whole family lineage passed down generationally. The higher Soul may break its silence and start shattering the pattern for everyone involved. This might create a lot of chaos and heartbreak at first, but people start taking their power back from the abusive patterns and heal generations forwards and backwards.

The dark secret comes to the surface and starts freeing everyone, even the perpetrators, freeing them because they have been caught or exposed and don't have the ability to harm or hurt others.

I know that was Frank's experience while he was in the coma. While I was on the plane back to Hawaii, I was meditating, and I saw him with his spiritual team in the Akashic record room. He was there deciding if he would return to the Earth or go home into Spirit. He made the choice to come back for a short time to complete and heal with everyone in love and that he did. When he left, he left in love and everyone on the Earth had the opportunity to heal with him, and he brought our whole family unit and all of his friends back in to One family of Love, forgiveness, and gratitude.

Frank had come back for a short week living from higher aspects of himself. He was absolutely living from his higher Christ I AM, and everyone who came in contact with him shifted into higher frequencies of Love.

I had an incredible experience with my friend, Julie, who is editing this book and who has edited all five of my books. After Frank passed, I contacted her to see if she would be able to edit my book with Frank. She responded that she was not able to assist with this one at that time. I thought it was because the book was about the death of my son, and she has two boys with whom she is very close.

I always write my book in longhand, not on the computer, and Julie must decipher my handwriting and type it up for me.

When I returned to Sedona with the intention to start writing the book, I felt lost. I had no idea who I could find who could help type and edit the book. Frank told me to contact Julie again, that she would change her mind and assist with the new book. And that she did.

Our first meeting together to go over the book was an incredible experience. Frank was very much with us and assisted Julie to shift into her higher, multidimensional self.

Julie Speaking

One of the hardest things I have done is tell Michelle that I could not participate in typing/editing her latest book. The subject matter did not deter me; my own personal grief process was in full swing as I moved out of a recurring life theme and left my job, friends and that life behind. I took the opportunity that summer to spend time helping my son and daughter-in-law with their new baby while my son went to school for his new nursing position. It gave me the opportunity to go within, not deal with any outside drama and chaos and address what I needed to change. This included losing 70 pounds and gaining self-awareness beyond measure and courage to begin again in a brand-new direction.

Yes, I am sure Frank was hovering as Michelle made the call again asking me if I was available to now type/edit her book. I was elated to do so and accepted immediately. When we met again at my house, oh my goodness, was Frank's energy filling the room! I described how he looked, and Michelle said that is absolutely how he presents himself to many others in her workshops. What a handsome surfer dude he is!

Before "they" arrived that day, I was preparing and noticed I was glowing in the mirror. The person staring back at me appeared radiant and very happy, which I am now, from the inside out.

After chatting for a bit and getting the back story of how Frank had passed, I felt chills because something similar happened to me on April 14, 2019 (one year and one day after Frank's passing). I had been given an antibiotic for a severe leg rash, possible MRSA infection and was unaware that it is not something I should ever be prescribed. Having ignored the instructions on the antibiotic paperwork (and still in my car), I started the medicine. Within a few doses, I was not feeling well but thought it was just killing the infection. While out in the sun the third day on the medication, I started feeling like I was about to faint and heard 1,000 cicadas in my ears. I knew I needed to sit down and get out of the heat. I had the wherewithal to turn off the water and walk over to the chair located on the cement pond area in my yard. I passed out and must have been out of it for almost 30 minutes. I awoke feeling very groggy, wondering why a chair was on my back and why I had gravel in my mouth. I went inside, took a time-stamp picture so no one would think my husband beat me (shocking I thought of that ... he was on a plane) and then off to bed I went. Three hours later, I sent the picture of my face all banged up to my ER nurse son who told me to get right to the ER and stop the medicine, which I did. He said I was not sounding at all like myself, and I could not even find the correct parking lot for the ER. Luckily, it turned out I did not have a fractured skull or concussion.

After chatting and catching up, Michelle and I took a walk around my fabulous Yellow Brick Road Homestead park for a bit after our initial greeting. It was grounding and felt really peaceful out there. Without any prompting from me, suddenly Michelle stopped walking and stood in the exact spot in my ½ acre yard where my head hit the pavement and I passed out. She said, "You mean where you died." I was shocked but felt the truth of what she was saying. And as I made the realization of what her words meant, Michelle's expression turned into one of utter surprise. She said, "I am watching your entire energy field shift. Your face is contorting. I don't even recognize who you are! I actually see you moving into the higher aspect of yourself as I am speaking!" Maybe my morning bathroom reflection was a precursor to what actually took place a couple of hours later!

This is how our latest adventure began - so much synchronicity and similarity with how Frank passed. I know beyond a shadow of a doubt that he was there for both of us and got us to a place of peace during our transitions to get to work on the new book. And so we did!

Michelle Speaking

A few weeks later, I was with Julie for a few hours. We were going over the book, and she had shown me some of the blankets that she had crocheted for others, for her family. Her crocheting is absolutely beautiful, and she captures the energy of the person for whom she is making the blanket.

As I was getting ready to leave, she said, "Just a minute. I want to show you a little something I have for you." She took me into her family room and said, "This is yours." I could not grasp what she was saying to me. Draped over the back of the sofa bed was the most beautiful king-sized, crocheted blanket that I have ever seen. Again, she said, "This is yours!" I was in shock. She said after I left, the day she shifted dimensions in her backyard, Frank asked her to make me a blanket. He had instructed her with the color choices of the blanket. The aqua for the new lifetime color; the gold for the Christ consciousness, green for Mother Earth; turquoise for Mother Mary; and throughout the blanket is purple for the I Am presence.

I was stunned. I could not believe that she would make me something so beautiful and that Frank was actually the orchestrator. Thank you, Julie, and thank you, Frank. This blanket is my heart, and I will treasure it for the rest of my days on the Earth.

As I look at the blanket, it is actually the colors of my first book *The Creator Speaks*. This book was surprisedly channeled through me from the Creator.

Julie's Walk-in Experience

Many things have changed in my life since that day Michelle visited and since I completed the 21-day process. So much fear has been released.

I am so much more courageous! Nothing scares me anymore; I just forge ahead and do what calls me like taking a mediumship class and not worrying about being the outcast who talks to dead people. Before that day, I was afraid I was giving and receiving messages incorrectly, that I wasn't good enough.

Now, I really don't care at all what people think of me, and nothing holds me back. The thought of not trying something new or getting in front of people is not even in my consciousness.

Timelines have been collapsing daily as the great shift is occurring. So many synchronicities occur where I speak a word and read that word at the same time.

My connection to my higher self, my angels, and my Spirit guides is deepening daily. It is so easy for me to give love, forgive, and be loving than ever before.

Also, I am just so much happier, calmer, and more relaxed with a deep sense of knowing that everything is all right.

Michelle's Walk-in Experience

As we complete out of the difficult cycles, our old consciousness leaves, and we expand into a higher consciousness of our Being. We have a higher aspect of our self walk-in and fill the space of the karmic aspect of our self that left.

I have gone through this process a few times in my life. Two of them are below.

My first walk-in experience was at 33 when I went through my first major breakthrough (breakdown). I was guided to the Holistic Health College, and a doorway of my higher calling as a healer flew wide open.

My second major walk-in experience was in 2004 when I went through my near-death experience (NDE) in India. I definitely shifted into a higher expression and expansion of myself.

When I returned to America, I channeled my first book *The Creator Speaks*. This book now is my fifth book. I am dyslexic and don't even read much, and I became as author.

Sallee's Walk-in Experience

I was in the movie theater with a friend watching a movie based on a true story. The movie was getting over when I felt the presence of a Being next to me, behind and to my right. My friend had gotten up to go to the bathroom. My next experience was my Heart opening like a fountain, and I watched in bliss as all this love poured out.

It was Michelle who told me that Spirit was showing her that this was a walk-in of a higher aspect of me. I do believe this because it was after this experience that I rapidly advanced spiritually and consciously. My frequency has become quite high, and I am continuing to move forward into my higher, spiritual work with Mary Magdalene, Yeshua, and my whole team.

Walk-ins / A New Soul Walked In

The other kind of walk-in is when another Soul actually comes into the original occupant's personality of the body.

When this takes places, both Souls are in the body for a period of 24 to 36 hours. The Soul coming in takes on the memory bank of the Soul that is leaving. It downloads the departing Soul's entire karmic agreements, emotions, what has been completed, and what still needs to be healed and completed.

The gift of this transition is the Soul leaving gets to have its karmic agreements completed for its willingness to leave and allow another Soul to occupy its body.

The gift for the Soul coming in is it does not have to go through all of the growing up stages to get to a place where it can make a difference in people's lives and in the world.

The Soul is already in a memory bank/personality of the Soul that is leaving. It has enough life experiences and knowledge to be able to go forward and teach others.

As the new Soul continues to clean up karmically for the original Soul, it now has enough wisdom to be able to assist others that have gone through similar experiences. It also has the ability to assist others to heal and shift into the light and gifts of these experiences.

This switch is always by agreement. Before the switch happens, both Souls come together in the Spirit world, in the Akashic record room, and design the whole set-up of what will take place here on Earth.

I was facilitating a workshop in the north of Sweden, and at the very end we were all holding hands in gratitude. We were listening to a song of completion when a woman in the circle fell down to the ground and passed out. I removed myself from the circle and asked the rest of them to continue.

I sat next to the woman who had fainted, and I received a message that a walk-in was coming in. This was another Soul exchanging places with the original Soul/personality.

When the woman opened her eyes and looked at me, she said, "I am not the same Soul that I was when I fell down here." I said, "I know that you are not the same Soul. I will explain it to you after the workshop is over."

What Happens to Dark/Shadow Souls When They Leave the Earth?

There is a dimension, a place where Shadow Souls go that have appeared to have failed their earthly mission. It is what some on your planet might call Purgatory. It is actually a holding dimension of the ego, of the Shadow.

The Shadow Souls come to this dimension after transitioning from Earth. It is a place where these ego Souls have all the different lessons that they have done to others, or themselves, constantly mirrored back to them. As the lessons are mirrored back to them, they feel the emotions of all whom they have harmed or hurt. There is no way for these Beings to turn away from this mirror experience. As they connect with other ego Soul Beings in this dimension, they experience what these Beings have done to others. They feel the collective emotion of fear, terror, control, injustice, grief, loss and abandonment. The Beings in this dimension go through this process constantly. The only way they are able to move away from it is to start feeling remorse. The mirror of this painful Shadow/Dark energy penetrates their whole Being until they feel like they are going to break, and break is what they do.

Their protective, fear structure begins breaking down until the Being starts understanding the pain and hurt it has brought to others. It is sometimes so overwhelming, the Being, or Soul, wishes it could die again to the place of non-existence. The Soul starts begging for forgiveness, and from this a true healing starts taking place.

There are many ascended Master, light Beings, whose mission is to come to this dimension and mirror the constant love and light of the Shadow Beings' magnificence to them. From this place, the Shadow Souls start to feel, heal, and return to the light. After many veils have been unthreaded, or released, the Souls leave this Shadow dimension and move into the higher dimensions to go through another healing process. After this great cleansing and rethreading back into balance, the Souls can then choose to once again reincarnate. Some of these Souls are so comfortable to be the Shadow's carrier that they choose to once again reincarnate in a Shadow lifetime. Many others choose to reincarnate as victims of the Shadow, or as a light Being or warrior, who comes up against the Dark or Shadow. The Soul feels it has an advantage and much understanding of the Shadow because it has vibrated in it so much. It understands the Shadow's mind, how it works, and the way it maneuvers in and out of the light.

Glossary

Akashic Records – a record of each Soul's individual journey from the beginning of its split from the One Soul

Ascension – the process of spiritual awakening that moves you into a higher level of consciousness

Chakra - "wheels" or energy centers found throughout our bodies that move energy and keep us functioning at optimal levels

Karma – In essence, the law that states that everything we do creates an effect that comes back to us – cause and effect. Much of what we are clearing and healing now is the effect from other lifetimes.

Third Eye – invisible, spiritual eye of God in the middle of the forehead. This eye provides perception beyond ordinary sight.

About Michelle

Michelle Phillips is an internationally renowned intuitive, healer, speaker, author and workshop facilitator. Her other books are: *The Creator Speaks, The Creator Teaches, The Creator Heals, and The Creator Archangels & Masters Speak on The Cosmic Ascension*. She has appeared on various radio and TV shows worldwide.

Michelle was born conscious of her gifts and always had a direct connection to the Source. She began her conscious spiritual work after healing her son from a severe kidney ailment. Since that Spiritual Awakening, she has dedicated her life to her spiritual purpose and mission, assisting others in their Soul's Awakening, self-love and purpose: co-creating Heaven on Earth in all life forms.

She refers to Christ as her "Main Man." From a very young age, He has been her, guide, assistant and teacher, He taught Michelle her spiritual work through her own healing experiences.

Michelle has been referred to as an Inter-Galactic Shaman because of her knowledge and ability to travel through many dimensions: Light/Dark, Shadow, Above and Below. She is known as the Healer's Healer. Many people come to Michelle as a last resort — when everything else has failed — and from her work, they experience life-changing transformations.

Her work includes:

- Workshops
- Soul Readings~Past Life Regression~Soul Retrieval~ Higher Self-Integration
- Inner Child Therapy~Childhood Trauma
- Relationship Issues~Twin Flame Healing of Imbalances

- Emotional Healings~Addiction~Health Issues~ Weight Loss

- Pineal Gland Activation~Reconnection to Creator

- Cellular Toning~Sound & Color Emotional Healing

- DNA Activation~Release~Repatterning*

- Sub-Personality~Entity Release

- Michelle is the developer and facilitator of the Christ Ray healing technique that she has taught worldwide.

Included in all of Michelle's private healing sessions and workshops is the reconnection to your higher self, Mother/ Father/Creator, and your inner children.

*The DNA repatterning came to Michelle after she was diagnosed with uterine cancer. She started looking at her family's genetic history and saw that her father seemed to carry many of the same health issues that she had gone through. She decided to travel energetically through her father's DNA, which had a profound healing effect. She then traveled through her mother's DNA, and then Mother/ Father/Creator's DNA. When she went in for surgery, not a trace of cancer was found.

Michelle is currently living in Sedona, Arizona. She is available to provide her experiential evenings, lectures, workshops, and private sessions worldwide. Michelle also offers long-distance phone sessions. Because her work transcends time and distance, a phone session has the same powerful experience and healing as if you had been with her in-person.

By participating in Michelle's workshops and private sessions, the areas of your life that hold you back, that create concern and conflict, will easily shift and change. You will experience great healing and changes in your mental, emotional, and physical bodies. You will shift unwanted aspects of your personality and release fears, phobias, low self-esteem, past difficult patterns and experiences, trauma, feelings of being unloved, loneliness, and many other imbalanced areas of your life.

For more information about Michelle, her work, or to request evenings, lectures workshops or phone session go to:

www.SoulsAwakening.com

Acknowledgements

I want to acknowledge Julie Carey for the many hours that she has spent assisting with this manuscript. I write everything longhand, and Julie has to decipher my handwriting and type it all up for me. We then spend many hours going back and forth with the manuscript, and Julie continues to edit to perfection.

This is the fifth book that Julie has done with me. I also want to thank her for her love and support.

I want to thank Sallee Eckert who spent many nights with me, helping me, holding my hand and holding the light for me as I, we, read through the book. I am grateful for her love and support as I reread the manuscript each time going through Frank's death again.

I also want to thank Mark Gelotte, my graphic artist. This is the fifth book we have done together. Mark is amazing. He absolutely captures the essence of what I want the cover to convey. He is also very humble, easy to work with, and very tuned in to Spirit. You can see more of his book designs at markgelotte.com

www.ingramcontent.com/pod-product-compliance
Lightning Source LLC
Chambersburg PA
CBHW031245090426
42742CB00007B/316